Jossey-Bass Teacher provides K–12 teachers with essential knowledge and tools to create a positive and lifelong impact on student learning. Trusted and experienced educational mentors offer practical classroom-tested and theory-based teaching resources for improving teaching practice in a broad range of grade levels and subject areas. From one educator to another, we want to be your first source to make every day your best day in teaching. *Jossey-Bass Teacher* resources serve two types of informational needs—essential knowledge and essential tools.

Essential knowledge resources provide the foundation, strategies, and methods from which teachers may design curriculum and instruction to challenge and excite their students. Connecting theory to practice, essential knowledge books rely on a solid research base and time-tested methods, offering the best ideas and guidance from many of the most experienced and well-respected experts in the field. Essential tools save teachers time and effort by offering proven, ready-to-use materials for in-class use. Our publications include activities, assessments, exercises, instruments, games, ready reference, and more. They enhance an entire course of study, a weekly lesson, or a daily plan. These essential tools provide insightful, practical, and comprehensive materials on topics that matter most to K–12 teachers.

To the WritersCorps family of teachers, youth, and staff
at the sites and to the creativity and community we've shared.

Jump Write In!

CREATIVE WRITING EXERCISES FOR DIVERSE COMMUNITIES, GRADES 6–12

Judith Tannenbaum
Valerie Chow Bush
WritersCorps Editors

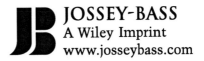

JOSSEY-BASS
A Wiley Imprint
www.josseybass.com

Published by Jossey-Bass
A Wiley Imprint
989 Market Street, San Francisco, CA 94103-1741   www.josseybass.com

Jossey-Bass books and products are available through most bookstores. To contact Jossey-Bass directly, call our Customer Care Department within the U.S. at 800-956-7739, outside the U.S. at 317-572-3986, or fax 317-572-4002.

Jossey-Bass also publishes its books in a variety of electronic formats. Some content that appears in print may not be available in electronic books.

Library of Congress Cataloging-in-Publication Data
Jump write in!: creative writing exercises for diverse communities, grades 6–12/WritersCorps; editors, Judith Tannenbaum, Valerie Chow Bush.
        p. cm.
   Includes bibliographical references and index.
   ISBN 13 978-0-7879-7777-1
   ISBN 10 0-7879-7777-2 (alk. paper)
1. Creative writing (Middle school). 2. Creative writing (Secondary education). 3. Multicultural education. 4. Children with social disabilities—Education. I. Tannenbaum, Judith. II. Bush, Valerie Chow. III. WritersCorps.
   LB1631.J86   2005
   808'.042'0712—dc22
2005013348

FIRST EDITION
HB Printing   10 9 8 7 6 5 4 3 2 1

Classroom teachers often feel pressure to choose between using standards-based lessons and activities that engage their students' creativity and encourage personal expression. In *Jump Write In!*, however, the experienced writer-teachers from WritersCorps offer numerous exercises that do both: build key standards-based writing skills and give voice to youth.

Through poetry, fiction, personal narrative, and playwriting, students will improve their writing skills by being invited to put their truths on the page. Perfect for a moment of improvisation as well as for deeper exploration, these easy-to-use and field-tested activities engage students from a variety of ethnic, educational, and economic backgrounds and encourage the recognition that their voices matter.

The book includes

- Dozens of exercises accompanied by teacher notes and suggestions
- Links to standards for each activity
- Examples of student work
- Suggestions for further reading

THE EDITORS

Judith Tannenbaum has taught poetry for the past thirty years. Her students have included primary-age children, maximum-security prisoners, continuation high school youth, and youngsters at a summer program for gifted teenagers. She has worked through California Poets in the Schools, California's Arts-in-Corrections, and UC Berkeley's Academic Talent Development Program and has also received several artist-in-residence grants from the California Arts Council. Judith has worked with San Francisco's WritersCorps since the program's beginning in 1994; she currently serves as training coordinator.

As editor, Judith created a prison arts newsletter for Arts-in-Corrections and the book *Manual for Artists Working in Prison*. She also wrote the *Handbook for Arts in the Youth Authority Program*. She has taught poetry in prisons in many states and has been keynote speaker at numerous conferences on prison and prison arts.

Judith has also written a book for teachers, *Teeth, Wiggly as Earthquakes: Writing Poetry in the Primary Grades* (Stenhouse Publishers, 2000) and a memoir, *Disguised as a Poem: My Years Teaching Poetry at San Quentin* (Northeastern University Press, 2000).

Valerie Chow Bush is a journalist and editor with more than thirteen years of experience. Her association with WritersCorps began in 1999, when she edited the youth poetry and prose anthology *What It Took for Me to Get Here.* She subsequently edited three books of poetry and prose by WritersCorps youth: *Smart Mouth, Jump,* and *Believe Me, I Know.*

Valerie was the executive editor of the *Media Guide to Islam,* an online primer for journalists covering Islam, Muslims, and Muslim Americans, sponsored by the Center for Integration and Improvement of Journalism at San Francisco State University in 2002. She was previously director of publications at the Maynard Institute for Journalism Education, an assistant editor at the *Village Voice,* and the executive director of the Asian American Journalists Association. Valerie received a master's degree from Columbia University Graduate School of Journalism.

Prior to becoming a journalist, Valerie was a community organizer in the battered-women's movement for nearly a decade. She is a cofounder of San Francisco's Asian Women's Shelter, one of the country's first multilingual safe homes for abused immigrant women and their children.

THE AUTHORS

Since its inception in 1994, WritersCorps has helped more than forty thousand people in some of America's most economically disadvantaged neighborhoods improve their literacy and self-sufficiency. WritersCorps has transformed the lives of thousands of youth at risk by teaching creative writing, giving voice to young people whose voices have been systematically ignored or disregarded. With its award-winning publications and national readings, WritersCorps has become a national arts and literacy model.

San Francisco, Washington, D.C., and Bronx, N.Y. were selected as the three initial sites for WritersCorps, chosen for their cities' exemplary art agencies with deep community roots and traditions of community activism among writers. In these three cities, WritersCorps established writers, working at public schools and social service organizations, and has helped people of virtually every race, ethnicity, and age improve literacy and communication skills, while offering creative expression as an alternative to violence and alcohol and drug abuse.

To learn more about WritersCorps contact

San Francisco WritersCorps
415-252-4655
www.writerscorps.org

D.C. WritersCorps
202-332-5455
www.dcwriterscorps.org

Bronx WritersCorps
718-409-1265
www.bronxarts.org

ACKNOWLEDGMENTS

WritersCorps gratefully acknowledges the support of the San Francisco Department of Children, Youth and Their Families; the San Francisco Department of Juvenile Probation; the Walter and Elise Haas Fund; the Richard and Rhoda Goldman Fund; the National Endowment for the Arts; the San Francisco Foundation; Working Assets; Northern California Independent Booksellers Association; and individuals. We recognize the San Francisco Arts Commission and its staff for their steadfast commitment to art for all people.

WritersCorps also thanks Judith Tannenbaum and Valerie Chow Bush for their work on this project, as well as WritersCorps teachers Cathy Arellano and Michelle Matz, who provided important feedback during the development of the manuscript. Thank you to David Fremont, Rick Rocamora, Katharine Gin, Bob Hsiang, and Lenny Limjoco for the use of their images and illustrations. Final thanks to all the WritersCorps teachers featured in *Jump Write In!* for sharing their great lessons and love for literature.

CURRICULUM AND STATE STANDARDS

This book, *Jump Right In!*, lends itself to assisting the teacher with specific activities to help meet standards for middle and senior high school, grades 6–12. Suggested activities for language arts, specifically those associated with literacy, have been keyed to the Standards for the English Language Arts, as determined by the National Council for Teachers of English (NCTE) and the International Reading Association (IRA). The standards address reading, writing, listening, viewing, and speaking, language, and literature. Because states vary widely in their specific definitions and in their nomenclature, the authors have provided broad guidelines based on national standards as footnotes to each chapter with the hope that teachers will derive these activities and will apply these suggestions to their lesson planning.

STANDARDS FOR THE LANGUAGE ARTS

The goal of the NCTE/IRA standards for language arts is to provide teachers with a framework to use with their students to foster communications and literacy skills. The standards address the following topical areas:

- Cultural issues and making meaning from a wide variety of both fiction and nonfiction texts (standard 1)
- Literature and genre concerns related to students reading a wide range of literature from numerous periods (standard 2)

- Interpreting, comprehending, evaluating, and appreciating texts through word meaning and textual feature recognition (standard 3)
- Adjusting the issues of spoken and visual languages and making language appropriate to an audience (standard 4)
- Including a variety of writing strategies (standard 5)
- Applying knowledge of language conventions and structures (standard 6)
- Conducting research on issues and generating ideas and questions from a variety of sources (standard 7)
- Using a variety of resources to gather and synthesize information (standard 8)
- Developing an understanding of diversity of language use (standard 9)
- Helping students use their first language (if this is not English) to understand curriculum content (standard 10)
- Becoming members of a literary community (standard 11)
- Using language to accomplish their own purposes (standard 12)

STANDARDS LINK

For the official NCTE/IRA standards for language, please visit the following Web site: http://www.ncte.org/about/over/standards/110846.htm

Key to Standards Used in *Jump Write In!*

Chapter Number	Standards Addressed
1	1,4,5,9,11
2	1,3,4,5,9,11
3	6
4	1,3–6; 9–12
5	1,3–6; 9–12
6	1,3,6
7	1,3,6,7,9,10
8	1,3–7,9,10
9	1–6; 8–12
10	1–7; 10–12
11	1–6; 9–12

CONTENTS

PREFACE

Since 1994 WritersCorps teachers have successfully helped students improve their writing, and thousands of great poems and stories have been born. One of the keys to teaching is a good lesson, and WritersCorps teachers have created hundreds. At each of our teacher meetings, a most valued outcome for teachers was to leave with lessons that colleagues had tested and offered.

WritersCorps created this book as a field guide to assist teachers who want their students to grow as writers. We invited our training coordinator, Judith Tannenbaum, to go through four years of teachers' notebooks, culling the best lessons and organizing these into a workbook for WritersCorps teachers. This workbook, *Lessons Along the Way,* enabled our teachers to find just the right lesson when entering an after-school center in the midst of a crisis, a classroom filled with middle school students sleepy after lunch, or the community room of a housing project.

Judith assembled and organized these lessons, and Valerie Chow Bush—who had edited four WritersCorps collections of student writing—shaped the manuscript into the most teacher-friendly format.

In 2004 Jossey-Bass gave WritersCorps an opportunity to revise our activity book and add new material. *Jump Write In!* represents the best practices to inspire teens and young adults to express themselves and create community through words. We hope that you will experience the positive outcomes we have when youth are encouraged to create their own literature.

INTRODUCTION

As teachers, you know that the young people who enter your classrooms are complex human beings who have much to say. Even a ten-year-old has lived through hundreds of happy and sad moments; every teenager already has her own dreams, fears, insights, and values. Each child has a unique way of seeing the world and speaks with an individual voice.

Since 1994 WritersCorps has created opportunities for urban youth to explore experience, observation, and emotion through the written word. Our teachers invite students to use their imaginations, express their feelings, and improve their skills while writing poems, stories, and plays. WritersCorps then shares the youths' creations in publications and readings, thereby allowing the larger community to learn from the lives and perspectives of our young people.

WritersCorps began in 1994, born out of discussions between Jane Alexander, former chair of the National Endowment for the Arts, and Eli Siegel, then-director of AmeriCorps, the federal national and community service agency that President Clinton created. Ms. Alexander's vision of using the enormous power of the arts to reach some of our country's most marginalized and underserved urban populations fit well into the AmeriCorps mission of serving U.S. communities.

In 1997 WritersCorps successfully made the transition from being a federally funded and administered organization to existing as an independent program, supported by a collaboration of public and private partners. In the city of San Francisco, WritersCorps continues to be a project of the San Francisco Arts Commission.

The program contracts with published writers who are also experienced teachers. These WritersCorps teachers join youth where they are: in public school classrooms, after-school programs, juvenile lockups, community centers, affordable housing projects, and the like. For many hours each week, for nine months of the year, often for a few years in a row, our teachers share the pleasures and skills of writing and also serve as mentors to their young students.

Most WritersCorps youth have had extensive experience with hardship; these experiences are part of who they are and what they bring to a writing workshop. Our teachers encounter moments such as the one Stephen Beachy faced when he arrived at his site in San Francisco's Tenderloin neighborhood. One of his students had recently attempted suicide, and all the youth in the room were agitated. Another young man said he was going to kill himself too. Stephen invited conversation, listened well, and then suggested that the group write a poem titled "Ten Reasons I Won't Kill Myself."

Corps teacher Godhuli Bose was equally attentive when a young student mentioned missing her daddy. Godhuli asked, "Where is your daddy?"

"In jail," was the girl's answer.

Godhuli told her student she missed *her* daddy too.

The girl asked, "Where's your daddy?"

"In heaven," Godhuli responded.

The two spoke back and forth until Godhuli felt the moment was right to ask her student, "Do you want to write a letter to your daddy?"

Even in moments less dramatic than these, WritersCorps workshops are most often composed of some students with minimal writing skills, others who read and write below their age level, and still others with so much to say that their pens barely lift from the page. The WritersCorps teacher always walks into a classroom, community room, or institutional dining hall having to figure out—as teacher Marvin K. White put it—"not the lowest common denominator, but the place we can all write from."

To determine "the place we can all write from" requires our teachers to have multiple gifts. They must have thorough knowledge of their subject matter, great concern for the youth they work with, and respect for staff at the sites hosting their workshops. Although the definition of metaphor and the purposes of personification remain constant, our teachers must recognize the difference between a sixth-period high school English class, a multiage neighborhood after-school program, and an evening workshop with incarcerated young men. Teachers make use of one kind of lesson when walking into the lounge of a drop-in center for runaway youth and another kind of lesson when meeting for the twentieth time with a consistent group of seventh graders.

WritersCorps teachers must be well prepared and also fully awake to students' needs in the moment. They must welcome unexpected opportunities, while firmly guiding students back to writing. They must have ground to stand on and, while standing, must be able to think on their feet.

Over the years WritersCorps teachers have created, developed, and used lessons appropriate to this wide range of demands. *Jump Write In! Creative Writing Exercises for Diverse Communities* is a compendium of these lessons.

Some of these exercises are tried-and-true classics, familiar to any veteran writing teacher. Many are adaptations, whether of an idea passed from teacher to teacher or of an exercise someone discovered in a creative writing book. Still others are pure invention, created, often on the spot, by a talented WritersCorps teacher. Despite their diverse origins, all the lessons you're about to discover share a common trait: a real teacher has field-tested each one with real students.

We recognize that you—as middle and high school teachers—must be alive to your students' needs while also addressing your state's standards and passing out grades. Still, WritersCorps and classroom teachers share a great deal. You also have days when tension vibrates through your classroom, afternoons when a student who hasn't shown up for weeks is suddenly there at her desk, mornings following a kid's death or arrest, and other class periods when your students are calm and able to focus. The lessons that follow are tools that you can use to help you respond to the human need of the moment, as you provide opportunities for your students to use and improve their writing skills.

We grouped the exercises into eleven chapters, from opening icebreakers to the process of editing nearly finished pieces for publication. Some lessons are what we call art attacks, exercises that offer an exciting onetime writing experience; others develop ideas and themes sequentially over a number of class sessions. We don't intend for you to teach these lessons in sequence, one after another. Instead, we suggest that you read through each section, picking and choosing the examples likely to work for you and your students.

The model poems sprinkled throughout are student work culled from WritersCorps teachers' journals, site chapbooks, and annual anthologies. They are suggested models and by no means the only examples you can use. We encourage you to seek out other model writing, whether student work, a favorite by a well-known poet, or your own writing.

The Further Reading sections that end some chapters will aid you in finding teaching ideas similar to those we've included. These references will also provide more information about the elements of poetry and teaching techniques.

We also suggest that you keep drawing materials on hand (paper, crayons, and markers), just in case. As WritersCorps teacher Susanna Hall put it: "It's good to always provide artsy materials for those who choose not to write because at least it keeps them at the table and in the discussion, and they can see and hear the writing that does get produced."

Teacher Marvin K. White noted that many of our students have strong negative feelings about anything related to school—even white, lined paper. Marvin's solution was to bring different objects for youth to write on: cardboard hearts, fluorescent paper, and brown paper bags, for example.

The lessons that follow bear the imprint of the urban youth with whom WritersCorps works. We urge you to consider factors such as your students' age, their familiarity with English, the length of time since they arrived from some other part of the world, and their living situation—whether a housing project, a prison, an apartment, or the street—as you choose lessons to teach.

In addition, individual WritersCorps members' teaching styles and intentions have shaped these lessons. Some teachers feel that the best writing comes from the direct encounter of one's senses with actual objects; others prefer to develop students' powers of imagination and memory. Some feel that young people are best served by starting off writing sessions with group discussions or brainstorms; others encourage students to go inward and trust what they alone see. One teacher wants students to follow a step-by-step set of directions; another leaves students free to respond to lessons as suggestions rather than mandates. Some teachers comment after students have read their poems; others offer a simple nod of the head.

We encourage you to adapt these lessons to the youth you work with, the realities of your school and community, and your own teaching style. We hope that you will make these lessons your own.

Icebreakers and
Opening Games

Building Trust

Trust between all teachers and their students, and between the students themselves, requires nurturing. WritersCorps teachers work with youth at sites from public housing to juvenile lockup and have found that a sense of safety rarely exists at the start of a workshop. Trust develops with time, as everyone gets to know one another, sharing challenges and triumphs.

Most of us need an atmosphere of trust and support to learn any subject. This need increases when the activity is creative writing, for such expression often requires emotional risk. A teacher must be certain that young writers feel safe before asking them to shape imagination into stories or to place memories and deep feelings into poem lines.

We're sure that you, as teachers, set clear expectations so that your students know they will be safe during classroom work and conversations. WritersCorps teachers too establish ground rules, discuss expectations, and raise issues of confidentiality. They do so in a manner most consistent with individual style. Some teachers prepare a poster of rules to hang on the wall; others create such a list with their students.

Whatever approach is appropriate for you and your students, it is important to recognize that inviting creative expression in your classroom requires that you pay heightened attention to

> **How often do teachers say "please" instead of "do the assignment"?**
>
> —High school student of WritersCorps teacher Beto Palomar

NCTE/IRA Standards
Standards 1, 4, 5, 9, 11

1

issues of privacy and trust. We can't stress too strongly that as the adults, we teachers must take responsibility for our students' emotional safety when we ask them to write about and then share feelings and personal experiences.

In the beginning WritersCorps teachers avoid asking students to write about sensitive topics, such as their fears, their worst memory, or their deepest loss. Instead, it is usually best to keep first sessions light and somewhat playful.

Reading one's own writing during the first session of a workshop helps establish the WritersCorps teacher as a writer and gives students a sense of the teacher's interests and styles. Such a reading also models a willingness to risk exposure— the very behavior that teachers desire from students.

Some teachers begin by having students write group poems because the process encourages teamwork and is less threatening than facing a blank sheet of paper on one's own. Others have students write individual poems immediately, allowing youth free expression. WritersCorps teacher Beto Palomar asks students to write him about what he needs to know about them to be their teacher.

Often teachers pass out writing journals when they first meet with students and give youth time to create collages on the journals' covers. This allows everyone to work on a nonthreatening and enjoyable project, encourages students to adapt a generic journal to their individual tastes, and validates each student's need for expression.

WritersCorps teacher Michelle Matz begins each class with a journal-writing session. She tells students that they can fold over the page they've written if they wish to keep their words private. Michelle tells students that in the five years she's been at their school, she's never once opened a folded journal page; she lets the youth know that she has the utmost respect for their privacy.

Michelle's invitation gives the young writers the power to determine whether or not they want anyone to read their journal entries. The youth feel the respect underlying Michelle's offer. Both this respect and the power of having a choice do much to encourage their trust.

Beto Palomar reports that students respond to his invitations to write. As one student commented, "How often do teachers say 'please' instead of 'do the assignment'?"

Michelle, Beto, and all WritersCorps teachers continue to nourish trust throughout the year by extending their students' right to make choices about their own writing. Which journal entries do they want to remain private? Which poem do they want to read to the class? And eventually, which of their writings do they want to publish?

SHIFTING THE MOOD

Even after establishing trust between the youth and between the youth and the adult, WritersCorps teachers often encounter students in moments of stress. Perhaps there has been an altercation in the lunchroom; perhaps the youth argued with her mother right before school; perhaps a child's father left home; there was a death in the family or a disagreement between friends.

WritersCorps teacher Jime Salcedo-Malo most often begins his workshops with an exercise designed to focus or to calm students. In a classroom of bored eighth graders, Jime dramatically recites one of his own poems by heart. With a small after-lunch workshop of thirteen-year-old girls, he leads a guided meditation that reconnects each student with her own imagination and capacity for peace. This shifting frees students for the writing ahead.

Some teachers use physical activity toward similar ends. As Gloria Yamato writes of her workshop with seven- to ten-year-old students at the Girls After School Academy: "I play with the girls, get into their rhythms, turning and skipping double Dutch. It pays off in workshop buddies and bundles of poems."

Instead of double Dutch, capoeira, or cartwheels, Gloria sometimes shares yoga with the girls to, as she puts it, "refocus on our bodies."

ICEBREAKERS: THE GREAT EQUALIZERS

Icebreakers or warm-up games are a great way to begin any class session—and not only the first gathering. They create a feeling of class cohesion, which is particularly useful when the youth come from a number of different schools. They're also effective when a teacher is working with a group of students who have varying degrees of English-language proficiency or when there's a substantial age range. "Warm-up games allow each student's voice to be heard in the beginning of each class," says WritersCorps teacher Michelle Matz. "This helps the quieter kids feel that there's a space for them too."

Here is an assortment of icebreakers and opening games that have worked for WritersCorps teachers. In general, opening games are longer than icebreakers and can easily lead directly into the primary writing exercise.

INTRODUCTIONS

Exercise
Are You Listening?

1. Students sit in a circle.

2. Each participant says his or her name and one fact about him- or herself.

3. Each person repeats what the person before has said.

Exercise
Lydia, Lion

1. Students sit in a circle.

2. Each person says his or her name and a word that begins with the first letter of that name—for example, "Simon, snake."

Exercise
Body Movements

1. Students sit in a circle.

2. Each student says his or her name and does a body movement (for example, placing a palm over the heart and then raising an arm to throw the heart's love into the room).

3. Everyone in the group repeats each name and body movement.

OPENING GAMES

Exercise Musical Chairs

1. Set up the chairs in a circle, setting out one less chair than there are participants.

2. Select a caller, who stands in front of the group.

3. The students then "number off": the first person calls out, "Lettuce"; the second calls, "Spinach"; the next calls, "Lettuce" again—continuing this sequence around the circle.

4. Everyone sits except the caller.

5. The caller calls out one of three possibilities: lettuce, spinach, or mixed greens. If she calls, "Lettuce," all those who had initially called out "Lettuce" must move from their seats and take one of the other vacated chairs. If she calls, "Spinach," all the spinach people have to move. If she calls, "Mixed greens," everyone must find a vacant chair, including the caller.

6. Whoever is left without a chair becomes the new caller.

Exercise Truth or Lie

1. In pairs, in small groups, or in the whole group, ask students to tell two truths and a lie. Because students are selecting which truths to share and which lies to invent, they have control over their degree of exposure. Still, we suggest that you choose this icebreaker only if your students are familiar and comfortable with each other.

2. If you want (and if you feel trust is assured), you can ask the group to try to spot the lie.

3. Ask the students to write a poem about the lie they told.

Exercise Card Charades

WritersCorps teacher Chad Sweeney created a version of the old party game of charades.

1. Ask a student volunteer to draw a card from a deck of cards.

2. The student then acts out the activity and the emotion of the chosen card, according to the following key:

Ace	Arguing with your parents
2	Brushing your teeth in a hurry
3	Playing a guitar for money
4	Walking a big dog in the park
5	Flying a kite in a strong wind
6	Waiting in line at a bank
7	Getting sick in an airplane
8	Riding a bicycle downhill
9	Walking home in the rain
10	Studying for a test late at night
Jack	Playing the piano at a famous concert hall
Queen	Blowing out candles on a birthday cake
King	Watching a movie with a special friend
Spade	Mad
Club	Scared
Heart	Happy
Diamond	Sad

For example, a student who draws a five of hearts must act out flying a kite in a strong wind and being happy at the same time.

Exercise Jeopardy

1. List six categories, such as emotions, colors, household items, geography, animals, and outer space.

2. Ask students to give an example for each category; list these words on the chalkboard or on chart paper.

3. When everyone has contributed words to each category, ask students to write a poem using any of the listed words.

WRITING WARM-UPS

Exercise Three-Minute Stories

1. Ask students to tell a three-minute story about a time when something amazed them. For example, WritersCorps teacher Kim Nelson begins by telling a childhood story of the time when her family came home from church to find that their seven canaries had escaped from the cages and were flying around the room.

2. The students can also write a poem or story based on their memories.

Exercise Sounds Like

1. Take a piece of paper and crumple it.

2. Make a list of things the crumpling paper sounds like (for example, rain, zipping a zipper, frying chicken, anger, a window breaking).

3. Students can write a group poem or individual poem based on this list.

Exercise A Pencil Isn't Just a Pencil

1. Students stand in a circle.

2. One student chooses an object in the room, such as a pencil, a yardstick, or a piece of paper.

3. The student names something the object might be. For example, the pencil might be a toothbrush, a cane for a very small person, or a long earring.

4. The student passes the object to the next person in the circle, who names something else the object might be.

5. Ask the students to write a poem using these metaphoric images (for information on metaphoric images, see Chapter Five).

Exercise Freewrite

1. Start a class session with freewriting. The rule is that anything goes. Ask students not to lift pen from paper and not to worry about spelling or grammar. Assure them that you will not require them to read their writing out loud, although they may choose to do so.

2. You can either give your students a prompt (see Chapter Four for ideas) or let them write about any subject that is on their minds.

3. After writing, ask students to circle a word in their freewrites that they like the sound or smell of, as in "I like the smell of hope."

4. Alternatively, you can ask students to circle five words from their freewrites and pass these words to the student on the right. Each student then writes a five-line poem with the words they've just received.

Writing in a Group

Time to Write

Icebreakers and opening games serve the useful purposes of focusing a group of students entering the classroom after

lunch, marking a transition from a formal lesson on a subject to the more open-ended writing exercises to follow, and allowing even shy students enjoyable group participation. Icebreakers are intended to be fast, fun, and easy; they encourage a light, lively mood.

As classroom teachers, you know how to assess the mood in your classroom and how to move students from one type of activity to another. You will find your own way—based on your students' needs and your own style—to shift from the quick pace of icebreakers to the slower possibilities of concentrated writing. Most WritersCorps teachers transition from icebreaker to writing lesson by inviting conversation on an interesting topic, proposing a prompt (see Chapter Four for a description of prompts), or reading an inspiring model poem.

THE VALUE OF WRITING TOGETHER

Sometimes the easiest and most comfortable way for students to begin writing is by working together: in pairs, in small groups, or as a class. Group writing breaks down students'

NCTE/IRA Standards
Standards 1, 3, 4, 5, 9, 11

> **These exercises help to demonstrate how elastic meaning is, how poems can emerge from random sources, and how they already exist in the world.**
>
> —Hoa Nguyen,
> WritersCorp teacher

reserve and fosters trust. Group exercises also allow you to assess your students' comfort level with writing and with being in the group on any particular day.

Even if you ask students to write individual poems or prose pieces, you can place such writing in a group context by beginning with a brainstorm on the day's topic. Or you can leave time at the end of the lesson for every student to read work aloud to the group.

COLLABORATIVE WRITING EXERCISES

Exercise *Group Poem*

1. Once you've brought up the day's theme through discussion, a prompt, or a model poem, ask participants to call out lines on the subject for a group poem.

2. Write these lines on the chalkboard or on chart paper.

3. Ask questions that encourage the youth to amplify their lines. For example, if a student says, "As sad as a king," you might ask, "What kind of king? What is that king doing?" This gives the youth a chance to describe the image more precisely: "As sad as a king alone on his throne."

4. Often students will repeat a form ("I felt as sad as . . . ") or elaborate on an image another student has described. "As sad as a man alone," one might say. "A man alone on the roof," another might add. "A man alone on the roof, whose eyes see beauty wherever they look."

5. When everyone has given a line, read all the lines back to the group.

6. Put the lines into a poem. You can do this in front of the group, describing your choices and modeling the process. Alternatively, the students can take on this task.

Exercise *Free Association*

This exercise works best with groups of about eight students who are familiar with each other.

1. Begin by explaining free association, for example: "I give you a word, and you give me a word in response."

2. Demonstrate the process with a student. Each person comes up with ten words to which the other person must respond. Keep a list of the twenty words that you and the student say.

3. Pair students up and have them free-associate ten words to make up a list of twenty words.

4. Students then write poems or stories based on their lists.

Exercise *Word or Sentence Layering*

1. Students sit in a circle so that the words can flow quickly.

2. Explain that each person will be responsible for adding one word or sentence to the story, spontaneously saying the first thing that comes into his or her mind, as in a free association.

3. The teacher or a selected student records the story as the group creates it.

4. One student begins by saying one word or a sentence, and each student adds another word or sentence.

5. The group decides when the story will end, but it should go on for a couple of pages.

6. The recorder reads the story back to the group.

Exercise *Write to Words and Drawings*

1. Ask students to write about the dumbest, goofiest thing they've seen recently or to write about what annoys them.

2. After everyone has written for two minutes, ask students to pass their papers to the person on their left.

3. Students then draw a picture based on what they read; after two minutes they pass the papers to their left, hiding the written portion. The students look at the drawings they've received and write about the picture for two minutes.

4. Repeat this process until each sheet returns to its original writer. Ask students to read the assembled stories, showing the illustrations.

Exercise Found Poems

This exercise helps—as WritersCorps teacher Hoa Nguyen put it—"to demonstrate how elastic meaning is, how poems can emerge from random sources, and how they already exist in the world."

1. Hand out newspapers or magazines and ask participants to look through them.

2. Students then call out phrases, words, or sentences from the newspapers and magazines.

3. The teacher or a student writes these words on the chalkboard or on chart paper and reads them back as a poem.

Exercise The Word Deck

1. Ask students to write down three words for each of various categories that you create (for example, foreign places, textures, sounds, colors, and foods).

2. Students choose their ten favorite words and write each word on a three-by-five-inch index card. Place the cards together in a word deck.

3. Pass out five cards to each student, and ask students to write a ten-line poem incorporating their five words.

Exercise Write from Five Words

1. Ask students to write down three words across the top of a blank piece of paper: a noun, a verb, and an adjective.

2. Then ask students to add two more words that don't seem to have any connection to the other three words.

3. Ask students to pass their papers to the person on their right and write a poem using the five words they receive. The students should also title their poems with words they didn't use in the text.

4. If there's time, they can repeat the process by passing the words to their left.

5. In another variation of this exercise, you choose a word as the title for a short poem. Each student writes a five-line poem with this title. When they're finished, ask students to pass their poems to the right. Now ask each student to choose one word from the poem he or she has received to use as the title for a new five-line poem. Continue until the original poems have made their way around the circle.

Further Reading

Hewitt, Geof. "The Unplanned Collaboration." In Christopher Edgar and Ron Padgett (eds.), *Old Faithful: Eighteen Writers Present Their Favorite Writing Assignments.* New York: Teachers & Writers Collaborative, 1995.

Poetry: A Primer

We encourage young writers to notice the difference in emotional weight between, say, "her smile is like the spine that centers my soul" (a simile) and "her smile is the spine that centers my soul" (a metaphor).

WritersCorps teachers encourage students to write stories, memoirs, and plays; and you will find lessons in *Jump Write In!* for each of these art forms. Poetry, though, is the genre that WritersCorps teachers most often share.

Of course, WritersCorps teachers tend to be poets themselves, so the particulars of poetics—image, sound, voice, line—are as familiar to them as the feel of your favorite red shirt is to you, as the smell of your baby girl when you kiss her soft skin, or as the taste of the cornbread your mother once baked. Poetry sings in these poets' souls. Poems are their bedrock, the thick quilt that comforts; poems are the water that a WritersCorps teacher pours over her summer-parched skin. A WritersCorps teacher spins similes ("as familiar as your favorite red shirt"), plays with personification ("poetry sings"), accents assonance ("flows from souls"), massages metaphors ("poems are the thick quilt that comforts"), and aligns alliterations ("poets play with personification").

WritersCorps teachers rhyme with their young rapping students and are able to freestyle on the spur of the moment. Our teachers are bards and can match beats with the best.

NCTE/IRA Standards
Standard 6

As a classroom teacher, you know what assonance is. You can give superb examples of extended metaphor and onomatopoeia. You know literature's vocabulary: abstract and concrete, allusion, cliché, free verse, image, meter, persona, point of view, refrain, stanza, voice, and the like. Such concepts are part of middle school and high school English–language arts content standards, and you use them in your classroom. Still, if you would like some vocabulary reminders, we've defined terms relating to image in Chapter Five and terms relating to sound in Chapter Six.

You can use the word *metaphor* and point out alliteration, but perhaps you don't think of yourself as a poet. Though you feel comfortable offering poetry's glossary, perhaps you're a bit shy about bursting into the song of a poem or maintaining the meter of lines that declaim.

That's OK. Just remember that inspiring your students to write poems—or stories, memoirs, or plays—asks that you share poetics not as a subject for a test but as a living art.

For example, conceits such as metaphor and simile are not static but lively. Instead of a drill on definitions ("*metaphor* is a figure of speech in which a word or phrase literally denoting one kind of object or idea is used in place of another to suggest a likeness between them"), we encourage you to ask young writers to notice the difference in emotional weight between, say, "her smile is like the spine that centers my soul" (a simile) and "her smile is the spine that centers my soul" (a metaphor).

Although we've created chapters on image, sound, and point of view, these elements live whole in a poem. Therefore, though you may find it useful—as do WritersCorps teachers—to focus on image in one lesson and sound in another, do be aware that any good poem gains power through image *and* sound *and* voice *and* line break and so on. The simple line we used earlier, for example, "her smile is the spine that centers my soul," makes obvious use of metaphoric image, assonance, and alliteration.

Also, as you're well aware, your students already bring their own understanding of poems into your classroom. Perhaps they memorized Langston Hughes's poem "Dream Deferred" in elementary school; perhaps they've read Shakespeare's sonnets; perhaps you have to remind them to remove their headphones in class and stop mouthing the words to the rap that's caught their attention.

Your students, of course, are the ones you want to encourage to write. Their histories, their loves and angers, the details that capture their interest—who they are— is always relevant.

Be open and curious about the poems you share, the exercises you offer, and the youth in your classroom. That's WritersCorps' best advice, our poetry primer.

Art Attacks

Prepare to Improvise

WritersCorps teachers often work in environments with high
student turnover. In the drop-in lounge of a center for homeless and runaway youth or at a juvenile detention facility,
WritersCorps teachers may meet with different young people
each week. In community centers and after-school programs,
participants may show up one week, disappear for three, then
return for the following two.

In such situations WritersCorps teachers cannot expect to
plan a writing workshop in which, for example, they present
the elements of poetry incrementally, session by session. The
lack of group continuity also means that teachers often don't
have the luxury of assessing each participant's skills, needs, and
interests.

As a result, teachers must often design each encounter with
the students as a complete writing experience or art attack,
a term that WritersCorps teacher Marvin K. White coined. In
this way teachers serve those who come to class only once, as
well as those who show up for a few weeks in a row.

The ability to adapt to students' needs on a particular day
is also essential. One student may be dealing with a family
member's death, while the nice weather outside may distract
other students. The following art attacks are portable exercises
that will help you to prepare a lesson quickly and improvise as
the teaching situation demands.

chapter FOUR

**When I woke up
this morning . . .**

NCTE/IRA Standards
Standards 1, 3, 4, 5, 6, 9, 10, 11, 12

PROMPTS: USE FIRST LINES AS CATALYSTS

Prompts can serve as effective catalysts for writing by jump-starting students' creativity and free-associative thinking. One quick way to begin a lesson is to throw out an opening line and let your students complete it by writing a poem or prose piece. You can make up the opening line or choose one from a poem, short story, or play. Some teachers like to select a line that speaks to some query or interest the students are discussing (race, family, neighborhood, and so on).

Here are some prompts or first lines WritersCorps teachers have used:

- Don't tell me . . .

- Don't ask me . . .

- When I look in the mirror, I see . . .

- The voices in my head are telling me . . .

- I wish I had . . .

- I wish I could . . .

- When I woke up this morning . . .

- You should never have forgotten this . . .

- I was not supposed to remember . . .

- I never thought . . .

- I am the kind of man (or woman) who . . .

- I'm scared . . .

- I see . . .

- In my past life I was . . .

The following is a student poem in which the prompt became the poem's title.

In My Past Life

I
was an elephant
running across the
plains of the desert
my feet pounded out
the hot beat
under the dry sun
In my past life
I was water
I came up from the ground in trickles
and rushed over
its parched surface
the zebras drank me
and gazelles
passed through me
In my past life
I was the sand
at the feet of the pyramids
I stuck to the toes
of the men who dragged
heavy rock over my back
In my past life
I was a beetle
and women picked me up
and put me into their pockets for
good luck
In my past life
I was a sound
I was the whisper of the mother
who put her child to sleep hungry
In my past life
I was the child
that watched my mother cry

because this was not the life she chose
But in her next life she will be the gazelle
and I will be the grass
and I will feed her and she will run free
away from the cold cement walls
who know her too well.

Gabby Cole, age seventeen

Exercise *I Come from a Long Line of . . .*

1. Suggest that students imagine themselves sitting in a room that holds everybody who has ever been part of their family. What do these people look like? Ask the youth to be specific, noticing facial features and body types. Which uncle smiles with his hands covering his mouth? How does the grandmother walk?

2. Ask students to notice what they have in common with the people in this imagined room.

3. If you feel that a prompt (such as the ones in the previous list) would be useful, suggest that students write "I come from a long line of . . ." and then continue, as one student did in the following poem.

Where I Come From

I come from a long line of
confusion,
a long line of
patience
and understanding myself
when there's no one who understands.
I come from
a long line
that never ends
but bends

to the right
and then to the left.
I come from a long line of
liars
and fakers,
a line of cutters
who step in front of me
in line
in a long line
where I come from.

Jennifer Robles, age sixteen

Exercise *Random First Lines*

This exercise not only gives students a prompt but encourages them to let the tone of another writer's work inspire their own. WritersCorps teachers have sometimes found that at first students complain about the line they've received and ask to trade it in for another. You can comply, but teachers suggest instead encouraging students to enter the feeling expressed in the words they received by chance.

1. Write individual sentences culled from poems or stories on index cards.

2. Pass these out randomly.

3. The line that a student receives becomes the first line of her poem, essay, or story.

Exercise *Lines from Books*

1. Spread books on a table and let the students look through them.

2. Ask students to choose one line as the first line of a poem or story and another to serve as a last line.

3. Ask students to write a poem or story using these lines.

What Color Is Anger?

1. Ask students to write a first line that names an emotion or feeling, then to add a color.

2. On the second line, ask students to describe what this feeling sounds like.

3. The third line should describe what it smells like.

4. The fourth line should describe what it tastes like.

5. The fifth line should describe what it looks like.

6. And the sixth line should describe what it feels like.

Prompts and Repetition in Litanies.

Most formally a kind of prayer consisting of a long sequence of chanted supplications and responses, litanies become in poetry a form using repeated lines that have an incantatory power. WritersCorps teachers have asked students to write litanies based on a variety of emotions and situations. Here's a basic format for such an exercise:

1. Give students one of the first lines from the prompts list (see the section "Use First Lines as Catalysts").

2. Ask students to complete the line and then repeat it at least ten times using different endings.

PROMPTS THAT STIR MEMORIES

If many of your students come from other countries, you can use these prompts as part of a group of lessons on the students' countries and cultures of origin, on their immigration experience, and on their new life in the United

States. Ask students to look at maps of their homelands before completing these exercises.

Exercise *I Remember . . .*

1. Offer students this beginning phrase, and ask them to complete the sentences with different endings.

   I remember . . .

   (Repeat five times with different endings.)

   In my country . . .

   But here . . .

   (Repeat three times with different endings.)

   I am glad to be here because . . .

   But I am sad because . . .

   (Repeat three times with different endings.)

2. Students can create a poem or essay using one or all of the first-line prompts or by combining them. In the following model poem, the student chose to repeat the prompt "I remember."

I Remember Ukraine

I remember the fish that my friends and family always caught. I used to put them back in the lake where we got them from because I felt sorry for the poor little fishes.

I remember the markets where my grandma and I used to always go to buy chickens, rabbits, and kittens.

I remember the birch trees that we always saw whenever we got to our street.

I remember the builders building the big houses that took ten years to build. All the time my friends and I used to go and play in those unfinished buildings.

I remember the cold windy snow pushing me back when I was trying to go forward.

Anna Zaytseva, age twelve

Picture This

1. Pass out sheets of paper on which you have drawn three sets of photograph-mounting corners, framing a blank space in which three photographs might appear.

2. Ask students to imagine this as a page out of their photo albums. One picture is of themselves as a baby. The second picture is of themselves now. The third picture is of themselves when they are ninety.

3. Ask students to write inside the three frames, as though taking a photograph with words. The first piece, inspired by the baby picture, might begin with the line, "When I was a child, I didn't know . . ." The current picture might begin with "Now I know . . ." and the last with "Looking back on my life, I know . . ."

WRITING FROM LISTS

By randomly connecting words or images, a student can sometimes create fresh associations and new twists on meaning—one of the jobs of poetry. Writing from lists is one easy way to experiment with that process.

Connect Word Lists

1. Ask students to write two lists on a piece of paper. One might be a list of nouns and the second a list of emotions.

2. Ask them to draw lines randomly connecting each word in the first list with a word in the second list. (See the figure for an illustration of what a finished sheet might look like.)

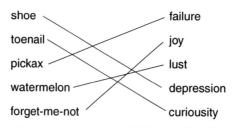

3. Ask students to write a poem using these randomly created "images." For example, they might write, "toenails of curiosity," "watermelons of lust," and so on.

4. To add a variation, you can have a group of students make up a list of their ten favorite words in Spanish or any other language common to the group. Using this list, they can write a poem or story.

WRITING IN FORMS

The words *poem, poet,* and *poetry* come from a Greek root that means "to make." Every poem is made. Every poem has a created shape.

Much contemporary poetry is written in free verse, without a fixed meter or line length. Sometimes the form's open possibilities intimidate young writers who appreciate the structure of writing in forms. "It seems that the more constraints I give students, the freer they are then able to be," says WritersCorps teacher Hoa Nguyen.

We suggest presenting even strict forms in the spirit of play rather than as an exercise in following the rules. You may offer haiku, for example, stressing the form's syllable count, and a student might write fifteen (rather than the traditional seventeen) syllables. Your student's lines might—as Basho, the seventeenth-century Japanese master of the haiku, put it—"Learn about pines from the pine, and about bamboo from the bamboo." In other words, your student's haiku might have accomplished the form's highest purpose. Please be amazed by the haiku, and worry some other time about this student's ability to count syllables.

Encouraging youth to respond to a poem, an idea, or a piece of art with his or her own writing is central to WritersCorps' intentions. As you share creative writing opportunities with your students, we urge you to focus more on your students' capacities for lively, engaging writing than on their ability to get a form precisely right.

ACROSTICS

An acrostic is a verse or arrangement of words in which a certain letter in each line, usually the first letter, spells out a word or phrase.

Exercise: *Write an Acrostic*

1. Begin the lesson by giving each student an envelope with one word printed on the front (for example, *peace, hope,* or *dream*). Inside the envelope place slips of paper printed with the individual letters that spell that word.

2. Ask students to write an acrostic, placing the paper slips, letter by letter, down the left side of the paper so that they form the word. The first line of the poem begins with the first letter; the second line begins with the second letter, and so forth.

Ode to the Motorcycle

O range stripes along the seat of it
D own the road to California
E nding in Los Angeles.
T o that long highway, where it is shining orange sunset over the highway.
O range.
T he gray helmet that he wears.
H eather on the back having fun.
E very day is an adventure.
M orning falls on the road. We drive again
O ver the winding roads
T ouring the cities we meet.
O n we go.
R ed helmet on my head.
C oming to the very end of the road.
Y ou're so pretty.
C oming to the very end, almost to California.
L ooking at the things I see
E nding in California.

Anonymous

HAIKU

Haiku, a form created in Japan, traditionally describes everyday experiences and uses direct language.

Many of us were taught that haiku must have seventeen syllables arranged in three lines in a five-seven-five pattern, but this isn't necessarily true. Many variations are possible—and allowable. Give your students the freedom to experiment. Haiku's ability to capture a moment in time and the form's use of direct language are often more important than its syllable count.

Young writers often intuitively catch on to haiku just by reading some. A good way to introduce the form is by reading the work of the Japanese haiku masters: Basho, Issa, and Buson. Students might also enjoy reading contemporary haiku writers such as Victor Hernandez Cruz, Etheridge Knight, and Ruth Forman.

For children from ages six to ten, WritersCorps teacher Alison Seevak suggests reading *Red Dragonfly on My Shoulder* (translated by Sylvia Cassedy and Kunihiro Suetake) and *Cool Melons—Turn to Frogs!: The Life and Poems of Issa* (by Matthew Gollub). Alison also recommends the Web site "Children's Haiku Garden." See the Further Reading section for publication information.

Exercise Word List

1. Ask students to list ten words related to a specific topic (for example, "my neighborhood").

2. Ask them to use these ten words to write a haiku. Don't insist that they strictly follow the traditional five-seven-five syllable count. Slight variations are fine.

Here are examples by three WritersCorps students.

Mother did not cook breakfast for me.
Maybe she was in a hurry.
Cold bread on the table.

Ming Cheng, age sixteen

The frog under red chairs
May soon spin on voices Ah!
More frogs carouse.

Ana Ramos

Sun and moon,
Bright and dark,
Again and again every day.

Joseph Beck, age eleven

Exercise *Someone Is Somewhere Doing Something*

1. Ask students to think about someone they know (for example, their mother, baby sister, grandmother) and imagine that person doing a specific activity (coming home from work, playing with a doll, cooking).

2. Ask students to keep this person and scene in mind and write a haiku in which the first line shows someone, the second line shows somewhere, and the third line shows that someone doing something.

WritersCorps teacher maiana minahal introduced the form to her students using as model a poem she herself wrote.

Father home from work
Rough hands at the piano
Caressing the keys.

maiana minahal

Please Mom come home now
In the kitchen cooking food
Fixing supper now.

Marlena Turner, age twenty

ODES

Odes come in many variations. The form dates back to the Greek poet Pindar, whose choral odes were sung and danced at public occasions. The form of the Pindaric ode—strophe, antistrophe, epode—directed the dancers literally to turn, counterturn, and stand. The tone of Pindaric odes is one of triumph and praise. English odes (primarily following the form of the Roman poet Horace) were not written for music. Twentieth-century odes are not always intended as pure praise. Many contemporary poets write odes, a form associated with triumph, with ironic overtones. (Allen Tate's work "Ode to the Confederate Dead" is one well-known example.)

Of course, it is not necessary to share this history with your students. But do keep in mind the form's traditional qualities. The ode

- Offers praise and celebration
- Often praises everyday objects
- Uses hyperbole
- Has an educational purpose (teaching us about objects)
- Elevates everyday life

Exercise Ode to Jell-O and Other Stuff

1. Introduce the ode to your students by reading a variety of odes such as those by Pablo Neruda, Gary Soto's *Neighborhood Odes,* or Lucille Clifton's poem "Homage to My Hips."

2. Ask students what they think the word *ode* means, based on the poems they just read. What do these poems have in common?

3. On the chalkboard or on chart paper, write the elements listed just before this exercise.

4. Ask students to think of an ordinary thing that they like and would want to write an ode to. One group of WritersCorps students, ages nine to twelve, wrote odes to Jell-O, hopscotch, and kickball.

5. If you feel that your group is ready for a more specific challenge, ask students to write an ode that teaches about the subject and persuades the reader of its importance, as two WritersCorps teenage students did in the following ode (with its fine examples of hyperbole and irony).

Ode to the Jerry Springer Show

Jerry, you keep me company
when I'm bored.
I like that I always know
where to find you.
I like it when the girls fight.
The guys just throw chairs around,
but the girls pull hair and slap.
Sometimes they take off their shoes
and throw them at each other.
I like how their hair gets messed up.
I like it when people from the audience
get down and fight and when
they get in fights with the guests.

I like it when the people say,
"Jerry, Jerry," as if you are fighting, too.
I like the way I know
my life is pretty normal
when I watch you.
And I like the way I know
I can always turn you off.

Alejandra Gamez, age fifteen
Arlene Ortiz, age twelve
With teacher Alison Seevak

RECIPES

Many WritersCorps teachers have discovered that students enjoy writing poems in the form of a recipe, using the vocabulary of measurement and instruction. Food is important in most cultures and is an accessible subject for even very young children. Food memories—cooking with Grandmother, savoring the aroma of her gumbo simmering on the stove—also serve as powerful catalysts for writing. Before you begin, bring in recipe books or magazines with recipes and ask the students to consider the words that recipes use and study the recipes' structure.

Exercise: One Cup of Creativity

1. Ask the group to make a list of words (nouns, verbs, and adjectives) used in relation to cooking: *heat, beat, boil, fold, simmer, cup, pound, sprinkles,* and so on.

2. Ask students, individually or as a group, to use these words and structures (including measurements) to describe themselves, school, the human race, their neighborhood, or any other topic of interest.

3. WritersCorps teacher Mahru Elahi plays Angie Stone's song "The Ingredients of Love" (*Mahogany Soul,* J Records, 2001) to augment this lesson.

Here are two examples of poems that students created from this exercise, each with a quite different tone.

Generations of Love

My grandma taught me to cook when I was seven years old and
    helping her.
Her mama taught her and her mama's mama taught her.
I want one of my recipes in a cookbook.
I like to cook lemon shrimp because it tastes crunchy, juicy, spicy,
    and tender.
Here is the recipe for Lemon Shrimp:
Buy five pounds of shrimp.
Put the shrimp in the flour.
Put them in the skillet.
Fry them for twenty minutes.
If you want them to be crunchy
then put in ½ cup of honey.
Add some pepper,
lemon spice,
one slice of lemon,
a few sprinkles of sugar,
and salt.
Then mix well,
and you have your sauce.

    Lorna Jackson, age eleven

Street

Four cups of sewer water (don't boil to make sanitary)
Eight pounds of just undercooked pork
with ten thin slices of processed "American" cheese
Five clean needles, along with twenty dirty ones
a couple of pimp hats, along with the snakeskin shoes
a dirty pound of crack, along with a failed dream or two
a baby who doesn't have a chance, and a mother who doesn't care
a white man with a white limo and a black hooker by his side
seven drops of dealer blood, and seven hundred haunting spirits
(optional) cheesy politician's campaign
Mold together into a shape not particular (any way it fits)
Bake in the oven at broil
It's ready when it's burned to a black, flaky crisp

Tara Somers, age sixteen

FUNKY CORPSE

WritersCorps teacher Russell Reza-Khaliz Gonzaga developed funky corpse based on a spoken word game he played as a teenager. It's a hip-hop version of exquisite corpse, a game invented by the French surrealists. In exquisite corpse the first player comes up with one line of free verse and passes it on to the next participant. The poem ends when it returns to the creator of the first line.

In funky corpse the poems must split the lines in *rhymed couplets,* two lines that rhyme and have the same number of syllables. Players can either take turns writing lines of a poem or orally improvise lines. If the players are skilled rappers, you may want to add the challenge of having them sustain a steady rhythm.

Exercise
Play Funky Corpse

1. Poet A writes a single line.

2. Poet B writes the next line, which must rhyme with the first line (near rhymes are fine).

3. Poet B then writes line three.

4. Poet C writes line four, which must rhyme with line three, and line five.

5. The poem continues around the group until it returns to Poet A, who completes the piece with a single line that rhymes with the preceding line.

Here's a model of a funky corpse by WritersCorps teacher Russell Reza-Khaliz Gonzaga:

1. We war with one another, killing sisters and brothers,

2. marching off to die, breaking the hearts of the mothers.

3. Politicians choose what is right, what is wrong,

4. have to have an enemy, have to have a gun.

5. Maybe you know how it hurts to see

6. the rich politicians' stupidity.

7. Life to them ain't nothing but a game,

8. "Shoot 'em down, draft some more"—will it always be the same?

9. This is the doom of the human being,

10. to the heart it hurts and to the soul it stings.

VILLANELLE

Forms such as the villanelle and sestina are intriguing but complicated. Many WritersCorps teachers have shared these (originally French) forms despite their structural intricacies.

The best way to teach a villanelle is to show an example of a successful one. Theodore Roethke's poem "The Waking," Dylan Thomas's work "Do Not Go Gentle into That Good Night," and Elizabeth Bishop's poem "One Art" are well-known villanelles and good models to use.

By looking at the model villanelle, you and your students can describe the form: a nineteen-line poem with six stanzas. The first five stanzas are three lines long (tercets), and the last stanza is four lines long (a quatrain). Two lines are repeated throughout the poem in a prescribed order. The tercet's rhyme scheme is ABA; the quatrain's is ABAA.

Additionally, you can use a template that WritersCorps teacher Kim Nelson created. Kim adapted a more open version of the form for the incarcerated young men she works with at Log Cabin Ranch. Noted on the template are the lines that will repeat and the lines that are open.

Here's Kim's template:

A1:   first repeating line
B: an open line—write what you wish
A2:   second repeating line

A: an open line—write what you wish
B: an open line—write what you wish
A1:   repeat line A1 unchanged

A: an open line—write what you wish
B: an open line—write what you wish
A2:   repeat line A2 unchanged

A: an open line—write what you wish
B: an open line—write what you wish
A1:   repeat line A1 unchanged

A: an open line—write what you wish
B: an open line—write what you wish
A2:   repeat line A2 unchanged

A: an open line—write what you wish
B: an open line—write what you wish
A1:   repeat line A1 unchanged
A2:   repeat line A2 unchanged

Exercise *Writing a Villanelle*

1. Start by reading a sample villanelle such as the ones by Roethke, Thomas, or Bishop. Ask students to identify the pattern in the poems, then hand out Kim's template so that they can see this pattern on paper.

2. Ask students to write two lines they would like to repeat or to choose a line from a poem or story they've already written.

3. Once students have their two lines (A1 and A2), ask them to plug these lines into the form.

4. Now ask students to fill in the open lines, trying to adhere to the villanelle's prescribed rhyme scheme.

Kim cautions that you may need to devote two class sessions to this exercise. Explaining the form individually to students often helps them understand how the pattern works.

Students may get frustrated by the fourth or fifth stanza, at which point the poem insists on its own direction. Kim handles this by discussing the value of letting the poem have some control, of pushing against the form and using the tension to the poem's benefit.

GETTING OUTDOORS

When the weather gets warm, students may have a hard time settling down to work inside. It may be a good idea to take your class outside and ask students to write about their surroundings. Not only will everyone get some fresh air, but going for a walk to observe and record the neighborhood and the people who live and work there can lead to important writing.

Exercise **Landscape and Memory**

1. Before your group leaves the building, talk about the five senses and, if you wish, read a model poem that uses sensory information. WritersCorps teacher maiana minahal, who developed this lesson, uses Donna Masini's poem "Giants in the Earth." If you read a model poem, ask participants to discuss how the poet uses the senses in the poem.

2. Take students outside and ask them, as they walk around, to write two examples of what each of their five senses notices (what they see, smell, taste, touch, and hear). Ask them to choose details they wouldn't normally notice.

3. Sit outside or come back to your meeting space and ask students to share at least one item from their list.

4. Ask students to write a piece using at least three items from their list.

Further Reading

Adisa, Opal Palmer. "Memory Is a Cozy Old Blanket." In Christopher Edgar and Ron Padgett (eds.), *Old Faithful: Eighteen Writers Present Their Favorite Writing Assignments.* New York: Teachers & Writers Collaborative, 1995.

Benun, Ilise. "Misery Is Fun: Using Langston Hughes's Black Misery." In Lorenzo Thomas (ed.), *Sing the Sun Up: Creative Writing Ideas from African American Literature.* New York: Teachers & Writers Collaborative, 1998.

Bishop, Elizabeth. "One Art." *The Complete Poems, 1927–1979.* New York: Farrar, Straus and Giroux, 1979.

Cassedy, Sylvia, and Suetake, Kunihiro (trans.). *Red Dragonfly on My Shoulder.* New York: HarperCollins, 1992.

"Children's Haiku Garden." [http://homepage2.nifty.com/haiku-eg/].

Clifton, Lucille. "Homage to My Hips." *Good Woman: Poems and a Memoir 1969–1980.* Brockport, N.Y.: BOA Editions, 1987.

Collom, Jack, and Noethe, Sheryl. *Poetry Everywhere.* New York: Teachers & Writers Collaborative, 1994.

Cruz, Victor Hernandez. "Haikukoos." *By Lingual Wholes.* San Francisco: Momo's Press, 1982.

Forman, Ruth. *Renaissance.* Boston: Beacon Press, 1997.

Espada, Martín. "Ode to Pablo Neruda: Using Odes in the Creative Writing Classroom." In Julio Marzan (ed.), *Luna, Luna: Creative Writing Ideas from Spanish, Latin American, and Latino Literature.* New York: Teachers & Writers Collaborative, 1997.

Fagin, Larry. "Memories." *The List Poem: A Guide to Teaching and Writing Catalogue Verse.* New York: Teachers & Writers Collaborative, 2000.

Gollub, Matthew. *Cool Melons—Turn to Frogs!: The Life and Poems of Issa.* New York: Lee & Low Books, 1998.

Knight, Etheridge. *The Essential Etheridge Knight.* Pittsburgh: University of Pittsburgh Press, 1986.

Masini, Donna. "Giants in the Earth." *That Kind of Danger.* Boston: Beacon, 1994.

Morse, Michael. "My Heart Fills Up with Hungry Fear." In Lorenzo Thomas (ed.), *Sing the Sun Up: Creative Writing Ideas from African American Literature.* New York: Teachers & Writers Collaborative, 1998.

Padgett, Ron, and Bill Zavatsky. "Gimmicks." In Ron Padgett and Bill Zavatsky (eds.), *The Whole Word Catalogue 2.* New York: Teachers & Writers Collaborative, 1987.

Raby, Elizabeth. "Teaching Etheridge Knight's 'The Idea of Ancestry.'" In Lorenzo Thomas (ed.), *Sing the Sun Up: Creative Writing Ideas from African American Literature.* New York: Teachers & Writers Collaborative, 1998.

Roethke, Theodore. "The Waking." *The Collected Poems of Theodore Roethke.* New York: Doubleday, 1953.

Soto, Gary. *Neighborhood Odes.* New York: Harcourt Children's Books, 1994.

Tate, Allen. *Selected Poems.* New York: Scribner's, 1937.

Thomas, Dylan. "Do Not Go Gentle into That Good Night." *The Poems of Dylan Thomas.* New York: New Directions, 1952.

Unger, David. "Antonio Machado's 'Childhood Memory.'" In Julio Marzan (ed.), *Luna, Luna: Creative Writing Ideas from Spanish, Latin American, and Latino Literature.* New York: Teachers & Writers Collaborative, 1997.

Images

Anger lives in a lonely cave where he even gets mad at the bats for making noises while he is sleeping.

—Saman Minapara,
age nine

Unleashing the Imagination

Poems and stories allow young writers to express their innermost feelings, insights, and thoughts. However, poems and stories are not simply forms of self-expression. Telling the reader that you have a particular feeling is the task of journal or essay writing. Creating the feeling for a reader is the poet's or storyteller's job; it changes simple expression into art.

Imagery is one of the primary tools at the writer's disposal to create an experience for the reader. Some images are literal or straightforward; others make use of figurative language, primarily metaphor, simile, and personification.

Young writers possess a wealth of image-making power, but they are often unaware of it or refuse to use it for fear of reprisal

NCTE/IRA Standards
Standards 1, 3, 4, 5, 6, 9, 10, 11, 12

from adults and peers. They have learned to carefully contain their imaginative powers. One of the biggest challenges that WritersCorps teachers face is finding ways to encourage students to tap into and trust their imagination and their senses.

WHAT IS IMAGERY?

Whatever your approach to introducing imagery in creative writing, you should touch on the following key points:

Although in common speech, the word *image* has visual connotations, in writing the concept means description—either factual or comparative—of something perceived through any one of the five senses. An image is a detail of sight, sound, smell, taste, or touch.

Point out that the word *image* is connected to the word *imagination.* Our imaginations have the ability to see, hear, smell, taste, and touch people, objects, and scenes not physically present.

INTRODUCING IMAGES

A simple way to approach images is through some kind of imaginative game. Ask students to close their eyes, then lead them through an exercise in which they "see" a reality different from that in the room around them. If it's a cold winter day, ask students to see themselves out in the park on a warm spring day. What are they wearing? What do they smell? What does their skin feel like? In other words, ask students to use all five senses in creating an imaginary scene.

Another basic approach is to discuss the imagery in a particular poem. The following student poem, for example, uses both straightforward and metaphoric images.

Sweet Bun

The bridge is pink with people crossing it.
It feels like wood under my feet.
The water is dark blue.
The bridge tastes like a round soft sweet bun,
the kind Chinese people make.
It smells like bread.

Lily Nguyen, age nine

DESCRIPTIVE OR LITERAL IMAGERY

Descriptive or literal images are factual, describing in words exactly what the writer sees, hears, smells, tastes, and touches.

Exercise Describe a Scene

1. Ask students to look closely at the room in which they are sitting and to gather information about the scene from all five senses.

2. Ask them to write a description based on their observations or to speak aloud to the group or to one person in the group, using straightforward descriptive language.

3. Now ask students to visualize another setting, one that's familiar but accessible only with their imagination or memory: their bedroom, the school gym, a specific street corner, the spot in the river where they fished with their grandfather in the country they came from.

4. Ask students to write a description of this place using straightforward language.

Exercise Describe a Known Object

1. Bring in interesting objects to place as a still life or display in the room.

2. Ask students to choose one object and write a factual description of it.

3. Alternatively, ask students to write about an object of their own, such as a jacket, ring, or tattoo.

Exercise Describe an Unseen Object

1. Bring in an object that you hide under a cloth or towel.

2. Ask students to touch the covered object.

3. Ask them to write a factual description of this object using the sensory information that they can gather.

Exercise Describe a Found Object

1. Go outside, preferably to a park.

2. Ask students to find one special object—a stone, feather, rock, or something else.

3. Ask students to look carefully at the object they've chosen and to write about it using straightforward language.

FIGURATIVE LANGUAGE

Figurative language makes connections between things we typically do not associate with each other. Because it allows for complex associations, figurative language enables a writer to express ideas and feelings that may not be literally true but are emotionally powerful.

Some major figures are metaphor, simile, and personification. A metaphor compares two unlike things by saying that one is the other. Pablo Neruda's poem "Ode to Watermelon" says of the watermelon: "It's the green whale of summer."

A simile also compares two unlike things but uses *like* or *as,* allowing the two objects to remain distinct but related. Robert Burns, for example, writes: "My luve is like a red, red rose."

Personification is a figure of speech that gives human qualities to inanimate objects. "Despair papered her bathroom walls with newspaper articles on acid rain," writes J. Ruth Gendler in *The Book of Qualities.*

Exercise Metaphor

1. Read the following examples of metaphor from students of WritersCorps teacher Chad Sweeney.

The stars are white fish swimming in the night sea.

My heart is a box that I open and close.

My soul is a river flowing from the mountains.

Love is the last fruit on an old tree.

Poetry is a horse running on a dark street.

My life is a wrinkled note dropped into the trash.

The moon is a pearl hanging from a necklace.

My mind is an open window with the wind blowing in.

2. Ask students: "What is a metaphor?" Ask questions such as "How is an open window different from a closed window with boards nailing it shut? What do these different metaphors say about the state of the poet's mind?"

3. Then read the following descriptions, which are not metaphors.

The stars are shining bright in the black night.

My heart is red.

Love is good.

4. Ask students to note the difference between the metaphors and the straight-forward statements.

5. Ask students to write their own metaphors, choosing one of the items in the earlier list (stars, heart, soul, love, poetry, life, moon, mind). Chad suggests that his students repeat the same opening phrase and write at least five different metaphors. He encourages his students to think of metaphors that no one has ever thought of before.

Exercise Describe a Person

1. Distribute copies of the following poem and read it aloud with your students.

My Family

My mom is a red rose blooming beneath the sunlight.
My dad is the grey cloud high above my head.
My sister is the newly budding carnation in the still of the night.
My brothers are the great white stars high up in the heavens.
And my grandmother is the bright yellow light that shines wherever I go.

Karen Macatuno

2. Ask students what Karen feels about these people in her family. Point out that Karen doesn't tell us "My grandmother is really important to me" but shows us what she feels through imagery. (This might be a good time to explain the difference between simile and metaphor. What subtle difference would there be if Karen had written "My grandmother *is like* the bright yellow light that shines wherever I go"?)

3. Ask students to write a series of lines—they don't have to compose a poem—in which they create metaphoric images for people they know well: family members, friends, enemies, or themselves. They will be completing lines that begin like this: "My best friend is . . ."

Exercise Describe Abstractions

1. Give students a list of abstractions (abstractions are general and the opposite of concrete): greed, love, homelessness, joy, death, beauty, and so forth.

2. Ask them to write either an image for each abstraction or several images for one of the abstractions. For example, they might write for homelessness: "The man curled in the doorway sleeps under his torn plaid jacket, hugging a teddy bear."

3. Ask students to write a poem or story that uses these images.

The following student poem develops a series of images of the abstract noun *death.*

Death Is

Death is like walking on a cloud.
The sharp feeling that tingles one's heart
is nothing compared to the soft
coffin that the dead lie on.
The splash of blood is stirred with tears.
The soul is held by bright hands.
The lost soul swims in the red fire.
The eyes cannot sparkle and can no longer tear
or the voice no longer sing. The body
is then sunk under the fertile soil
that Carlo walks on.

Carlo Gascon

4. If you feel that your students need more direction, you can prepare a list of questions they can ask about the abstraction. For example:

- What does anger taste like?

- If you could wear anger, what type of clothing would it be?

- What kind of machine would anger be?

- If anger were a noise, what would you hear?

- If anger were weather, what would it be like?

- If anger were a car, where would it take you?

- If anger were an animal, what would it be?

5. You can also ask students to imagine an abstract value as a place and write about it. For example, what if freedom, creativity, or fear were a place? What would that place look like?

Exercise *I Am Making a House*

This exercise, created by WritersCorps teacher Chad Sweeney, aims at developing figurative images in the familiar terrain of the house. It also focuses students on what shape they want their lives to take in the coming years.

1. Ask students to brainstorm a list of household items, rooms, parts of a house, for example: window, toaster, bed, kitchen, door, fireplace, garden, and so on. Write twenty or thirty of these words on the chalkboard.

2. Ask students to write a poem in which they build their own fantasy house. Read the poem that follows before students begin to write. Chad wrote this poem specifically to use in this lesson; you might write your own model poem for your students.

The House

I am making a house
with my own two hands.

I am making a house with windows
of blue glass
looking out across the whole world.

There is a special place
for my mother to sit in the garden
and watch the birds flying in circles,
the mimosa trees full of purple flowers.

There is music coming from the walls,
the rhythms of Mexico,
the songs of China,
and the joy of Africa.

I am building a house with love,
where everyone will be welcome,
people from all nations,
a bed to rest their bodies after hard work.

The house has a magic kitchen
where the tamales and rice
taste so delicious
and a banana tree offers new bananas every day.

There are books beside every chair,
magic books that speak and tell their stories,
books where the pictures move
with horses and rivers.

At night I sleep in warm water
or a hammock suspended in the air
or on the fresh spring grass.

My house is constructed from poetry
from dreams
from the roots of many mountains.

Exercise *Magic Senses*

WritersCorps teacher Chad Sweeney asks his students to explore the senses through both literal and metaphorical images in this exercise.

Our actual senses know the world through specific, interesting image detail, for example: "With my hands I can feel the rocky soil in my grandmother's garden and the cool of her wedding ring."

"Magic senses" may use a blend of sense or mental processes, for example: "With my magic hands I can touch the soft memories of my grandmother and the broken music of the moonlight." Or "My magic tongue can taste the stillness of the air in Grandmother's house the day she died and the first lemonade she made for me years ago."

1. You will be asking students to explore their actual senses with specific detail and to explore magic senses with metaphor. Magic senses are not bound by time and space. Use this format or some variation.

   With my hands I can feel (or touch) . . .
   With my magic hands I can feel (or touch) . . .

or

> My hands can feel . . .
> My magic hands can feel . . .
> My eyes can see . . .
> My magic eyes can see . . .
> With my tongue I can taste . . .
> With my magic tongue I can taste . . .
> My ears can hear (listen to) . . .
> My magic ears can hear (or listen to) . . .
> With my nose I can smell . . .
> With my magic nose I can smell . . .

Here are some student poems you might use as models.

> My eyes
> see the beautiful colors
>   of the rainbow
>   after the rain.
> My magic eyes
> can see the sound
>   of the flower's
>   heart.
>
> Blanca Trejo, age sixteen

> With my ears I can hear the brakes
> of the cars on the street.
> With my magic ears I can hear fish
> moving
> in the sea.
>
> Yan Cai, age fifteen

Exercise *In the Postcard*

In this exercise students also use both literal and metaphorical imagery.

1. Bring in a selection of postcards with interesting images.

2. Ask students to select one that intrigues them.

3. Ask them to describe the colors, people, animals, or actions in the postcard. You might prepare a list of questions, such as

- What is happening?

- What is about to happen?

- Where are you?

- What can you see, hear, smell, taste, and touch?

- Who else is there with you?

- What do you wish would happen?

- What don't you want to happen?

- What can you see in the story that you can't see in the picture (what is hidden)?

Here is a student poem inspired by this exercise.

Glass with Water

there's a room in summer
and a glass with water
standing, sitting on a table
a little boy with a button nose
reaches for it.
fingers on glass
glass w/ water wants to
play and run like the boy.
the boy spills water from the
glass.
the glass feels like floating
in an ocean of darkness
glass w/ water never full
never empty wanting to be gulped
like mad love, swallowed
whole by some strange woman's
nice hot lips on cold glass w/ water
glass w/ water steaming like
a bathroom window

Debbie Landeros, age eighteen

4. In another variation of this exercise, ask students to imagine that they are in the photo. They can pretend to be anything—the sky, a person, a tree, a dog. Let the students write for five minutes, then have them pass the photos to their right. Each student then writes about a new photo for five minutes.

Exercise *Describe Color*

1. Bring in objects with distinctive colors or swatches of colorful cloth or paint.

2. Ask students to write a poem or story in which they describe one of the colors—the color, not the object—for a blind person.

Exercise *Extraordinary Objects*

1. Bring in a number of objects (hat, paper, apple, pencil) or ask students to look around the room and notice the objects within it (flag, people, clock).

2. Show a hat, for example, and ask students to brainstorm comparisons: a flying saucer, a basket, a mushroom, and so forth. Write these on the board or on chart paper.

3. Ask students to write figurative images for one of the objects.

One WritersCorps student came up with the following powerful metaphor for a car.

Car
A sparkling beached ship, that travels on black seas.

Armando Aguilar, age fourteen

Exercise *Dear Pillow*

1. Tell students that they'll be writing a letter to a person they don't know or to an object they know very well.

2. Write suggestions on the board or on chart paper. Tell students, for example, to write a letter addressed to any of these:

- Your tired feet

- Your bad memory

- The street, house, city, or country you lived in when you were younger

- A grandparent or relative you've never met or barely know

- A celebrity you love or hate

- A politician you love or hate

- A favorite item of clothing

- A favorite possession

3. Read a model poem by way of example, such as the following by a Writers-Corps student.

Dear Bed and Pillow,

I am writing to let you know how much you mean to me. You two are the ones that listen, understand, and give me rest. Whenever I am in trouble or have a love problem, you are the ones that are always there to listen to me. When I tell you guys about what's wrong with me, you guys don't blame me or tell me what to do. That's one of the many things that I love about you. You are the best friends that I ever had. As a matter of fact, that's why I take care of you and try to keep you two clean and healthy. I love you guys so much that I don't let anyone else sleep on you. The two of you are mine and only mine. I am afraid that if someone sleeps with you they won't take good care of you. You two really deserve the best of the world.

Anonymous

Exercise Personifying Emotions

This exercise, based on J. Ruth Gendler's work *The Book of Qualities*, is a great way to introduce personification (giving human qualities or actions to inanimate objects or abstract ideas). You might read some of the entries from Gendler's book as models.

1. Brainstorm a list of emotional qualities: pleasure, fear, loneliness, judgment, wisdom, doubt, power, creativity, longing, and so on.

2. Ask students to choose one of these qualities and to imagine it as a person. If anger were a person, would it be male or female? What colors does anger like? What kind of food? What does anger spend its time doing? Who does anger hang out with?

3. Ask students to write a poem in which they personify the emotion they've chosen.

4. You may choose to read the model poem below before your students write.

Anger

Anger lives in a lonely cave
where he even gets mad at the bats
for making noises while he is sleeping.

He wears a shawl around his shoulders,
sits on rocks, and spits in a bucket,
talking to himself because he's lonely.

He has black eyes, a fierce face,
red hands, and crooked yellow teeth,
with a mouth scrumped up into a grrrrr.

Anger does not have a wife
because he does not want to be responsible
for someone else,
so he scares them away.

Anger dreams of having friends,
not always being cruel and nasty,
but when hope flutters by his window
he closes the curtains.

Saman Minapara, age nine

USING PROMPTS TO SPARK IMAGERY

Exercise *Metaphors for Myself*

1. Give students a list of questions to help them come up with metaphors for themselves. For example, ask them what season, color, action, or sound they are.

2. Ask students to respond to these questions in one-line answers on a sheet of paper.

3. Ask students to then write a poem or prose piece using one or all of the lines from their list.

Here is a list by a WritersCorps student, followed by the poem he wrote from it.

If I were a season, I would be winter.

If I were two colors, I would be maroon and forest green.

If I were two actions, I would be full of rage and mysterious.

If I were three sounds, they would be silence, mellow, and low.

If I were three things in a building, they would be floor, couch, and bed.

If I were three rooms, they would be the bedroom, the living room, and the garage.

Inside

You walk inside myself and it is winter on a dark night.
Not summer nor fields of wildflowers.
It is a huge field of rolling winds.
You follow the sound of emptiness
And you climb a stairway of mystery and curiosity
Made of just pure thoughts.
You are in my emptiness.
You have your peace.
The loneliness is a privilege.

Mikael La Torre

Exercise *I Am*

1. Ask students to close their eyes and visualize what they might compare themselves to—an animal, a place they feel safe, weather, a color or food they love.

2. Read the following model poem to the students.

I AM

I am the ghetto slums
drug sellin' baby boy who
thought the squeaky closet
was a ghost
I was the weed smoke
lingering in my lungs
the excitement that
picked up the gun
I am the choice that took
my freedom from me
the rain that sprinkled on me
I am the dream
that will one day be
free

Lawrence W., age seventeen

3. Point out the chantlike quality of the model poem (all those lines beginning with "I am"). Also, Lawrence does not say he is *like* something but that he *is* that thing. (This is another natural place to explain the technical terms *simile* and *metaphor*.)

4. Ask students to write "I Am" poems using their own images.

Exercise *Bragging Poem*

1. Ask students to brainstorm a list of sights, tastes, and smells that are extremely pleasing to their senses. Write these on the board or on chart paper.

2. Ask students to write a bragging poem in which they compare themselves to words on the list.

Exercise The Metaphor Résumé

1. Ask students to visualize a person, real or imagined, then distribute sheets of paper on which you have written:

If This Person Were

A vegetable	he or she would be a . . .
A car	he or she would be a . . .
A type of musical instrument	he or she would be a . . .
An animal	he or she would be a . . .
A piece of clothing	he or she would be a . . .
A color	he or she would be . . .
A foreign country	he or she would be . . .
A type of shoe	he or she would be a . . .
A weather condition	he or she would be a . . .

2. Ask students to write a poem based on their responses, such as this one.

Wilbur

If Wilbur were a vegetable, he'd be a freshly uprooted potato covered with soil.

If Wilbur were a musical instrument, he'd be an antique piano in desperate need of tuning.

If Wilbur were a type of shoe, he'd be a loafer with a lucky penny stuck to the inside.

If Wilbur were a weather condition, he'd be a mild, partly cloudy morning.

Carla M. Hill

Exercise Special Object

In this exercise WritersCorps teacher Chad Sweeney asks his students to imagine that a fire destroys their house. They have time to save one thing as they run out the door. What will they save?

1. Ask students to describe the object: What does it look like? What does it feel like in your hands?

2. Here are some other prompts:

How long have you had this object?

Who gave it to you, or how did you first get it?

Who made it, or where did it come from?

Why is it important to you?

If you lose it, can you buy another one?

Does the object have a special meaning for you? Please explain.

3. Ask students to write a short poem of thanks to the object. Here is one example poem by WritersCorps teacher Chad Sweeney.

To My Flute

Thank you for staying with me,
for never complaining when I needed
your song.

Thank you, flute, for being strong
as the cedar tree
from whose wood you were born.

Thank you for listening
to my sadness
in your hollow stomach.

Thank you for carrying my father's voice
and the Cheyenne spirit
and the wild Oklahoma wind.

Exercise *My Soul*

1. Pass out a list of prompts, such as the following:

My soul

moves like . . .

dreams about . . .

smells like . . .

feels like . . .

has been seen . . .

walks with . . .

is as . . . as . . .

Maybe my soul is . . .

Every day my soul . . .

2. Ask students to write poems about their souls, using the list of prompts. You can use the following poem as a model.

My Soul

My soul is a hollow-boned winged creature
with feathers soaring through blue skies
sometimes losing a beautiful colored feather.

My soul is jumping fences
sleeping through the winter winds
chasing cars and roaming in the wild.

Chrissy Adams

Further Reading

Barnett, Catherine. "Square Toes and Icy Arms: How to Simplify While You Personify." In Lorenzo Thomas (ed.), *Sing the Sun Up: Creative Writing Ideas from African American Literature.* New York: Teachers & Writers Collaborative, 1998.

Collom, Jack, and Noethe, Sheryl. *Poetry Everywhere.* New York: Teachers and Writers Collaborative, 1994.

Gendler, J. Ruth. *The Book of Qualities.* New York: HarperCollins, 1988.

Willis, Meredith Sue. "Mr. Death." In Christopher Edgar and Ron Padgett (eds.), *Old Faithful: Eighteen Writers Present Their Favorite Writing Assignments.* New York: Teachers & Writers Collaborative, 1995.

Sounds

Savoring the Sounds of Words

At the core of repeating and replicating sounds is the pure pleasure of the aural aspect of language. Many teachers choose to begin with that pleasure. Students may already equate poetry with particular sound qualities such as rhyme (the repetition of the same or similar sounds) and meter (a regular pattern of stresses). In fact, many WritersCorps youth favor rap music, the

lyrics of which most often follow a pattern of rhyme and meter. Students may be less familiar with other aspects of sound, such as assonance, alliteration, and onomatopoeia, which this lesson defines.

It's up to the WritersCorps teacher to decide when to go with and when to resist students' attraction to rhymed and metered verse. Many teachers have brought to class lyric sheets of rap songs and talked about form through the use of this familiar and valued musical genre. Other teachers feel that students are already knowledgeable about rhyme and meter, so they choose instead to focus primarily on the imagistic qualities of poetry.

Many books have excellent material on metrical matters, including scansion (the process of noting the metrical patterns of lines and stanzas). See the Further Reading section at the

> **I am the wind that blows your window curtains apart, the wind that blows the leaves off the trees and onto the dry grass.**
>
> —Anthony Mejia,
> age thirteen

end of this chapter for material about iambs and dactyls, hexameter and pentameter, if you want to share such information with interested students.

WRITING TO MUSIC

In most cultures poems were originally sung. Asking students to write to music connects them to poetry's roots. The pure sound of wordless music is particularly useful, providing a less logical, more magical source of inspiration than words or ideas.

Exercise *Freewrite to Music*

1. Bring in many tapes or compact discs, each with a different sound, or ask the students to bring in their own CDs and tapes. You can deepen the exercise by choosing music that reflects a variety of cultures.

2. As the students listen to the music, ask them to freewrite. Remind them that their pens should not leave the paper and that they should not edit themselves as they write.

3. Ask students to go over their freewrites to find lines that can serve as an entrance into a poem or story. Then have them write such a piece.

Exercise *Theme Songs*

1. Play songs with a particular theme. For example, one WritersCorps teacher used songs about summer by DJ Jazzy Jeff, Bob Dylan, Nat King Cole, Conjunto Cespedes, and the group Earth, Wind & Fire.

2. Ask students to listen to how each song portrays summer.

3. Discuss what they heard. What was the rhythm of summer? What was the tone? What images came up?

4. Ask students to write a poem or story based on the sensations and images these songs conveyed.

Exercise *Write the Blues*

1. Introduce the blues as a form of poetry. You might want to read up on the blues as a poetic form (see the Further Reading section).

2. Start by reading a blues poem or the lyrics of a blues song so that students can see the form's use. Some examples include "Homesick Blues" by Langston Hughes, "Blues" by Sonia Sanchez, and Sterling Brown's "Tin Roof Blues."

3. Play a variety of blues songs. Ask students to listen carefully to the rhythm and the repetition of lyrics. Ask which lines repeat and how that repetition makes the listener feel. Some songs you might play include "Give Me One Reason" by Tracy Chapman (*New Beginning;* Electra, 1995), "Blues Never Die" by Koko Taylor (*I Got What It Takes;* Alligator Records, 1975), "I Got the Blues" by poet Jayne Cortez (*Cheerful and Optimistic;* Bola Press, 1994), and "Howling for My Baby" by Howlin' Wolf (*The Essential Howlin' Wolf;* House of Blues, 1995).

4. After the discussion ask students to write blues poems, using material from their own lives. Encourage them to be specific about what gives them the blues.

Here's an example to use as a model poem if you wish.

Wake-Up Blues

When I wake up in the morning, I feel so down.
I say when I wake up in the morning, I feel so down.
Will I go to school? I don't really know right now.
What does it take to be awake?

I say what does it take to be awake?
A strong cup of coffee would be really great.
Let's start today in a different way.
I say let's start today in a different way.

I'm gonna turn over on my pillow and that's where I'm gonna stay.
When I wake up in the morning, I feel so down.
I say when I wake up in the morning, I feel so down.
Will I go to school? I don't really know right now.

Lester Nhan, age eighteen

REPETITION IN CHANTS

Chants are similar to litanies (see Chapter Four). Like litanies, chants also rely on repetition and have spiritual connotations. In Chapter Four we suggested writing litanies as quick art attacks. Here we emphasize the sound qualities of chants.

Poems in which part of a line repeats over and over have particular power. The rhythm of the repetition creates a musical beat that gives the chant a hypnotic sound far removed from common speech. Chants, often associated with prayer, should be read aloud. Blues songs, prison work songs, and slave songs trace their roots to the chant.

Exercise **Write a Chant**

1. Find a model chant you like, perhaps N. Scott Momaday's poem "The Delight Song of Tsoai-talee." The primary repeating line in Momaday's poem is "I am."

2. If possible, find a recording of such a chant. Listening to a chant being recited gives students the best sense of the form. One good example is the Mazatec *curandera* Maria Sabina on "Mushroom Ceremony of the Mazatec Indians of Mexico" (Smithsonian Folkways Recordings, 1957). If you use this recording, you might also want to read Anne Waldman's poem "Fast Speaking Woman." Sabina's chants inspired Waldman to write this poem.

3. Make sure that students notice the repeating lines of the form.

4. Ask students to write their own chants using a repeating line, either one from the model chant or one you give them.

Exercise **In Praise of the Body**

1. Create a deck of ten word cards for each student in your class by writing the names of different body parts (nose, head, elbow, backbone, and so on) on individual three-by-five-inch index cards. It's a good idea to choose the body parts yourself, thus avoiding any sexual or scatological references.

2. Ask each participant to select five cards from her deck.

3. Ask students to write a chant using the words on their cards:

Praise my head because . . .

Praise my feet because . . .

Praise my nose because . . .

Praise my spirit because . . .

Praise my backbone because . . .

ONOMATOPOEIA

Onomatopoeia is the use of words whose sounds express or imitate their meaning, such as *hiss, buzz, bang, rumble,* and *clatter.*

Exercise *A Fistful of Coins*

1. Ask students to really listen to the sounds around them: the shaking of a fistful of coins, the buzz of the fluorescent lights, the roar of the bus outside the window, or the thump of your work boots as you walk across the wood floor.

2. Ask students to brainstorm for words that convey the sounds they've been noticing.

3. Ask them to write a poem about coins or buses or work boots using some of the words the group has come up with.

ALLITERATION

Alliteration is the repetition of an initial consonant in near or neighboring words in a line or lines of verse.

Exercise *Peter Piper Picked a Peck*

1. Read examples of lines that use alliteration. You might choose examples from the books listed in this chapter and from your own reading, or you might use the following examples from poems by WritersCorps youth (both

published in *Believe Me, I Know,* 2002 WritersCorps anthology): "backs of burdens" (Marjon Kashani), "clouds of contamination" (anonymous).

2. Point out that tongue twisters depend on alliteration. Ask someone to recite a tongue twister ("Peter Piper picked a peck of pickled peppers"; "She sells seashells by the seashore").

3. Ask students to write some alliterative lines.

ASSONANCE

Assonance is the repetition of vowel sounds in the words of a line or lines of verse.

Exercise *Aeh, Oh, and Ee*

1. Point out the use of assonance in any poem you choose or in the following stanza:

I am the wind
that blows your window curtains
apart, the wind that blows the leaves
off the trees and onto the dry grass.

Anthony Mejia, age thirteen

2. Ask students (singly or in pairs) to go over a poem they've written, noting the use of assonance they find.

Further Reading

Boyd, Melba Joyce. "The Music in Afroamerican Poetry." In Lorenzo Thomas (ed.), *Sing the Sun Up: Creative Writing Ideas from African American Literature.* New York: Teachers & Writers Collaborative, 1998.

Brown, Sterling. "Tin Roof Blues." *The Collected Poems of Sterling Brown.* Chicago: Triquarterly Books, 1996.

Collom, Jack, and Noethe, Sheryl. *Poetry Everywhere.* New York: Teachers and Writers Collaborative, 1994.

Corn, Alfred. *The Poem's Heartbeat: A Manual of Prosody.* Ashland, Oreg.: Story Line Press, 1997.

Deutsch, Babette. *Poetry Handbook.* New York: Barnes & Noble, 1982.

Fussell, Paul. *Poetic Meter and Poetic Form.* New York: McGraw-Hill Higher Education, 1979.

Henriquez, Aurelia Lucía. "Be-Bop-Bo-Duh: Writing Jazz Poetry." In Lorenzo Thomas (ed.), *Sing the Sun Up: Creative Writing Ideas from African American Literature*. New York: Teachers & Writers Collaborative, 1998.

Hollander, John. *Rhyme's Reason: A Guide to English Verse*. Boston: Yale University Press, 1989.

Hughes, Langston. "Homesick Blues." *The Collected Poems of Langston Hughes*. New York: Vintage, 1995.

Logan, William Bryant. "Sound, Rhythm, Music: Using a Poem by Nicolás Guillén." In Julio Marzan (ed.), *Luna, Luna: Creative Writing Ideas from Spanish, Latin American, and Latino Literature*. New York: Teachers & Writers Collaborative, 1997.

Lowe, Janice. "The Delicate Rumble of Pianos: Using the Work of Bob Kaufman." In Lorenzo Thomas (ed.), *Sing the Sun Up: Creative Writing Ideas from African American Literature*. New York: Teachers & Writers Collaborative, 1998.

Mayes, Frances. *The Discovery of Poetry*. New York: Harcourt Brace Jovanovich, 1987.

Oliver, Mary. *A Poetry Handbook: A Prose Guide to Understanding and Writing Poetry*. New York: Harcourt Brace, 1994.

Oliver, Mary. *Rules for the Dance: A Handbook for Writing and Reading Metrical Verse*. Boston: Houghton Mifflin, 1998.

Mills, David. "*Ritmo y vida*/Rhythm and Life: A Voyage with Lorca." In Julio Marzan (ed.), *Luna, Luna: Creative Writing Ideas from Spanish, Latin American, and Latino Literature*. New York: Teachers & Writers Collaborative, 1997.

Momaday, N. Scott. "The Delight Song of Tsoai-talee." *The Gourd Dancer*. New York: Harper & Row, 1976.

Padgett, Rod. *Handbook of Poetic Forms*. New York: Teachers & Writers Collaborative, 1987.

Sanchez, Sonia. "Blues." *Like the Singing Coming Off the Drum: Love Poems*. Boston: Beacon, 1999.

Steele, Timothy. *All the Fun's in How You Say a Thing: An Explanation of Meter and Versification*. Athens: Ohio University Press, 1999.

Turco, Lewis. *The New Book of Forms*. Lebanon, N.H.: University Press of New England, 1986.

Waldman, Anne. "Fast Speaking Woman." *Fast Speaking Woman*. San Francisco: City Lights, 1975.

Narrative

The Art of Telling a Story

A narrative tells a story and can be written in poetry or prose. Whether the form is autobiographical writing, fiction, a dramatic scene, or a narrative poem, storytelling involves ele-

ments of plot (the pattern of events), setting (the time, place, and circumstances), character (the people), and dialogue (what the characters say).

Many exercises you've read thus far in *Jump Write In!* focus on writing short poems that typically deal with a single subject and are in the writer's own voice. Such exercises are most appropriate for many WritersCorps students and sites.

However, when the setting is right—as your classroom may be—WritersCorps teachers often choose to present exercises that allow students to write longer, more discursive narratives in both poetry and prose.

Human beings are storytelling creatures, and your students are likely to enjoy writing narratives. These exercises also encourage youth to speak from perspectives and experiences other than their own, thus expanding their sense of the world and their use of imagination.

I've been about everywhere and seen about everything there is to see . . .

—Anonymous

NCTE/IRA Standards
Standards 1, 3, 6, 7, 9, 10

EVERY OBJECT TELLS A STORY

Exercise *Still Life*

1. Set up a still life with interesting things to look at.

2. Let students handle and explore the objects.

3. Give students one minute to start writing a story.

4. When the minute is over, ask them to fold the paper over the lines they wrote, except for the last line, and pass the paper to the person on their right.

5. Ask students to read the last line on the papers and pick up the story from there, writing for one minute.

6. Tell students when the line they are writing will be the story's end.

Exercise *A Personal Possession*

1. Ask your students to bring in a personal possession they're willing to show to the class.

2. Place all these objects on a table.

3. Ask students to write a story in which they incorporate all the items.

FINDING THE STORIES AROUND US

Exercise *Tell Someone Else's Story*

Because this is one of those exercises in which students may respond by putting each other down, you should use caution in introducing it. Even if you're sure that all your students will react appropriately, refer explicitly to the ground rules about respect, trust, and safety that you've already set (see Chapter One). If you don't feel confident that your students can assure each other's emotional safety, it's better to skip exercises such as this one.

1. Ask students to pair up.

2. Each student tells his partner a story about something that really happened to him.

3. Ask each student to write his partner's story.

Exercise *What's My Story?*

1. Ask students to write a story about who they are.

The following example by a WritersCorps student is painful. Of course, the youth we work with often have painful stories, and writing about their pain is both honest and helpful because it allows the young writers to shape and contain what has been hard in their lives.

Still, WritersCorps teachers—always conscious about the issues of emotional safety we raise when we ask students to write—most often offer exercises such as this one in a way that encourages youth to make their own choices. The young writers can write stories that are painful or celebratory, amusing or intense, depending on their own desires and levels of comfort and trust.

My Life

I wasn't always in a computer class. Before that, I was living with my boyfriend in Berkeley who kicked me out of the house. Let's see, what's next? I used to live in about thirty-eight foster and group homes since I was thirteen. I've been about everywhere and seen about everything there is to see, done about everything there is to do, experienced every kind of kinky sex act except scat play. Done all the alcohol thing, done the drug thing, been in mental hospitals, been in rehabs, done the suicide thing, been homeless, been not homeless, fell in love, fell out of love, had boyfriends, had girlfriends, seen death, not seen death, looked death in the face, seen what an addiction can do, seen what an addiction cannot do, been walked on, walked on people, done that too. Never had a home, probably never will. Been pregnant, not been pregnant, been loved, not been loved, watched my friends with AIDS die, watched them live. Done the survival sex thing, not done the survival sex thing, stayed in a homeless shelter, not stayed in a homeless shelter. Been with girls, been with guys, watched people shoot up, not watched people shoot up. Been abused, been abusive, been raped, lived safely, not lived safely. Like I said, there isn't anything I haven't done.

Anonymous

Exercise Visualization

This is another exercise that requires some degree of trust and comfort on your students' part.

1. Ask students to walk around the room silently, avoiding physical or eye contact with one another.

2. As they walk, lead them through visualizations such as these:

    You are walking through deep mud in the middle of a jungle.

    You are walking on sand on a warm and glorious day.

    You are walking through a light mist that brushes your skin.

3. Encourage students to project the situation using their whole bodies.

4. Next, guide them through a more developed situation, such as this:

    You walk into a fancy Italian restaurant. (Ask them to act this out.) The waiter is slow to bring you a menu or wait on you. (Ask students to show their reactions physically.) Finally, he brings you soup. You're hungry because you have not eaten all day. Suddenly, he drops the soup in your lap! (Continue the story as long as you wish, making it as funny or dramatic as you desire.)

5. Ask students to choose one of the situations they just reacted to and to write a story about it.

6. After they have written for a minute or so, tell the students to have a character speak within their story.

7. After a few more minutes, ask students to make something unexpected, amusing, or exciting happen in their story and have all the characters react to it.

8. After a minute more, encourage them to have a character speak again.

9. After students finish their stories, encourage them to read the end result.

Exercise The Neighborhood

1. Take students out into the neighborhood.

2. Ask them to pair up and to pick a number between one and five, along with a letter—N, S, E, or W. The number is the number of blocks that that pair of students will walk; the letter is the direction they will take (north, south, east, west).

3. Tell them that their destination will be the setting for their story and that each person they see at their destination will be a character in their story.

4. Together, the pair determines the plot, the year in which the story occurs, and the place in the plot that the story will begin. Tell them to return to a designated spot by a certain time (for example, you can give them from five minutes to twenty minutes to observe and take notes).

5. Back at your site, have the pairs work together to write a story.

Exercise *Choose a Situation*

1. Write at least ten situations on one set of index cards. Write at least ten occupations on another set of index cards.

2. Ask students to choose one card of each type (a situation and an occupation).

3. Ask students to write a story involving a character with the occupation they selected, in the situation they selected.

Exercise *Story Shuffle*

1. Have students pair up.

2. Ask each student to write two one-page stories. The first story is about an early childhood memory, and the second is about a day on public transportation.

3. Ask the students to cut each story into separate lines and place the lines in one pile, then shuffle them.

4. Each person in the pair takes half of the pile, then pieces them together into a complete story.

Exercise *Five Minutes Before*

1. Bring in postcards.

2. Ask the students to choose one of these cards.

3. Ask them to imagine what happened five minutes before the photographer took the shot and to write a story about that moment.

Exercise **Finish the Story**

1. Start reading a narrative (for example, a short story, children's book, or chapter from a novel).

2. Stop halfway through.

3. Ask the students to finish the story, either by brainstorming as a group or writing alone.

Exercise **Those Familiar Places**

1. Ask the students to call out any familiar places they feel strongly about (their bedroom, a favorite café, and so on).

2. Give each student an envelope that contains a portrait, photo, or drawing of a person.

3. Ask the students to write a short story that incorporates one of the settings they've called out with the person whose picture they've received.

Point of View

Writing from a Different Perspective

When writing narratives—whether in the form of a story, poem, or personal essay—a writer must be conscious of *point of view*, the perspective from which an event is seen and related. Remind students that the "I" of a poem or a story may or may not be the

author herself. In either case, the writer's or fictional character's experiences, values, and attitudes all shape his or her point of view.

One way to introduce point of view is to talk about the concept in terms of visual art. You might stand or sit so that your students are looking at you from various places in the room. Ask them to pretend that they are drawing your portrait. Point out that even if every one of them had equal skill as an artist, their drawings would be different because each student would have drawn you from a different angle of vision. For example, one artist would draw the left side of your face, another the right side, a third would draw your portrait straight on.

You can expand this discussion by mentioning an event—preferably one that has taken place at your site. Discuss the

> **Right now a man sitting on a bench is laughing, a woman is giving birth to a boy in a car, a girl is getting caught stealing from a store, birds are flying around the park . . .**
>
> —Christina Duculan,
> age fourteen

NCTE/IRA Standards
Standards 1, 3, 4, 5, 6, 7, 9, 10

event and point out how, even when everyone tells the truth, each person's truth varies based on attitudes about the participants, awareness of the context, the amount of the event each person witnessed, and so on. Because each observer has a slightly different point of view, the resultant reports necessarily vary.

Of course, you will often want your students to write from their own points of view, but it is also useful and challenging for them to write from another person's or character's perspective. Breaking out of the first-person, purely autobiographical voice can expand imaginative power, writing skills, and compassion.

WRITING IN ANOTHER PERSON'S VOICE

The idea of writing in a voice or from a point of view not their own may bother some students. They may feel that such a voice is inauthentic because they believe that individuals can know and write only about their own experiences. Assure your students that there is a long and respected tradition in poetry and prose of pretending to be someone else, adopting a persona. Of course, novels would not exist without the creation of characters, each with his or her own point of view. Persona poems take their name from the Greek word for "mask."

Let students know that writing from someone else's perspective—in another voice—can be a great way to stretch imagination and writing style. Ask those who are still resistant to simply experiment.

Exercise *Write About Portraits*

1. Bring in portraits (on postcards or from magazines) of a variety of faces.

2. Ask students to choose one that interests them.

3. Ask students to write a poem from this person's point of view. Remind them that they are not writing their opinion about this person, but rather imagining how the person pictured sees the world.

Exercise *Shifting Perspective*

1. Ask students to write about someone that the entire class would know or at least recognize from another person's point of view. (Ask that this speaker

not be themselves.) For example, they might write about the mayor from the point of view of a homeless woman living on the streets of their city.

2. Then ask students to write about this subject in the first person, from their own point of view.

Exercise
Creating a Character

WritersCorps teacher Chad Sweeney says that the following activity shows students how central character development is to the plot of a story.

1. Ask students to answer the following questions in complete sentences. Point out that their answers will begin to tell a story; they can think of these answers as a rough version of Chapter One of a book they might write.

Where and when was the character born?

Who are his or her parents?

What jobs do they do?

Are they rich or poor?

What situation do they live in?

Who was the character's first friend?

What did they like to do for fun?

What makes this character different from other children?

Tell us about a major event that happens to your character at age ten.

Tell us about her or his first boyfriend or girlfriend.

Tell us about one time when the character was hurt or escaped from danger.

What special abilities does the character have?

What is he or she bad at?

Does the character tell the truth?

To whom does he or she sometimes tell a lie?

What does the character most want in life?

2. Using what they know about their characters, ask students to begin a sentence with the following: "Everything changed when . . ."

The Person Behind the Portrait

1. Ask each student to pick a partner. One person poses while the other draws her portrait. Then have students switch roles.

2. Ask the students to put all their drawings on the table.

3. Each person chooses a picture, preferably not of himself.

4. Ask students to create a new character based on this portrait. They should give the character a name and brainstorm about the character, listing her personality, life events, physical description, and so on.

5. Ask students to write a story or poem from this character's point of view.

A Parent's Voice

1. Read pieces written in a mother's voice. Some possibilities are "Emergency Situation" by Hal Sirowitz or "From Mother to Son" by Langston Hughes.

2. Ask students to write in the voice of a mother, father, or grandparent (their own, if they wish).

If you wish, you can ask students to write what the adult speaker of the piece has to say to its writer, the student, as in the following example.

How They See Me

Every conversation I have with you costs me money. Do we have a tree outside with money on it? You have over twenty pairs of shoes and I never see you wear the same thing twice. You need a job working from eight to five because you cost a lot. I feel sorry for your future husband because the only words you will tell him are "I want to have my hair done" and "I need money to buy weave." Every time you take pictures, I don't get one to carry around in my wallet. My friends ask me, "Do you have a picture of your daughter?" I say, "No, but I am the one who pays for it."

Jacqueline Andrea McKinney

Exercise *You Don't Know Anything About Me*

1. Bring photos from books or magazines. Make sure some faces are of teenagers, others of middle-aged adults.

2. Ask students to choose two photos, one from each age group.

3. Tell students that the photo of the older person is the teenager's parent and that one of the two has a secret, such as being gay, being an alcoholic, or being secretly in love.

4. Ask them to start their pieces with the words, "You don't know anything about me."

Exercise *A Baby's Perspective*

1. Ask students to write from a baby's perspective, inside the womb. (You might play Jimi Hendrix's song, "Belly-Button Window.")

2. You can expand on this exercise by asking students to write from the baby's point of view at ages two, five, and ten.

Exercise *In the Here and Now*

1. Ask students to brainstorm for examples of events occurring at that moment and list these on the chalkboard. Ask them to be specific and give details (for example, "Right now a seven-year-old is licking a double-dipped rocky road ice-cream cone").

2. Ask students to write a poem in which they imagine what is happening in the world right now.

Here's an example by a WritersCorps student.

What's in a Minute
Right now a man sitting on a bench is
laughing, a woman is giving birth

to a boy in a car, a girl is getting
caught stealing from a store, birds
are flying around the park, a
beetle is crawling on my book,
my brother is out with his
girlfriend kissing on the bus,
I'm all alone sitting on a bench
thinking about what to write,
somebody is running away from
home, an old lady just got hit
by a truck while trying to cross
the street, a white house is
burning, a girl fell off the
monkey bars, somebody
is committing suicide, a boy
is getting jumped by three guys,
somebody is taking a cold
shower, somebody is eating.

Christina Duculan, age fourteen

Exercise *What the Table Told Me*

1. Ask students to choose an object in the room, such as a chair, table, or chalkboard.

2. An alternative is to ask students to bring objects from home that are meaningful to them or ask them simply to remove the contents of their pockets.

3. Put all the items on a table and ask each student to choose one object.

4. Ask them to write a story or poem from the object's perspective. What does the object have to say? What is it observing, smelling, and feeling?

Here's one student example.

What the Table Told Me

The table told me he wants people to rub him down with that good-smelling stuff, and not with those rough napkins with our bare hands, because after all, we all need touch daily.

The table wants us to quit slamming things such as our hands, books, and pens on him just to get our points across. The table told me he hates it when we put our oily bags and hair on him; he's not in the kitchen or in a classroom. The table thinks it's silly and degrading that all of our chairs don't match. Well, actually, the chairs told the table, who told me. The table claims he's a male, and he likes when we wear shorts so he can see our legs. I told the table, "Don't be looking at us." And he told me, "Well, find something more for me to do."

Myeeka Calhoun, age twenty

Exercise *An Animal's Perspective*

Here's one way to make thinking about point of view more accessible to younger children. You could do a similar exercise with objects and people as well as animals.

1. Sit in a circle.

2. Ask students to pick an animal they would like to pretend to be.

3. Ask students to step one by one into the center of the circle and show how the animal moves, how it eats, and what kinds of sounds it makes.

4. After the student is finished performing, the other students guess what animal she was pretending to be.

5. Then the demonstrating student tells the group how old the animal was and where it lives—in the wild or inside a house.

6. Next, give students profile sheets with the following questions:

   What is your animal's name?

   How old is your animal?

   Who is in your animal's family?

   What does your animal wish for?

   What is your animal scared of?

   Where does your animal live?

7. Ask students to fill out these sheets, thereby developing more information about their animal characters.

8. If they wish, students can draw a picture of the animal and its home on the back of the profile sheets.

9. Ask students to write a story or poem using these profiles. Prompt them by suggesting that they could write a story about a time their animal wanted something and tried to get it, either succeeding or failing in the process.

Exercise *Write Monologues*

1. Ask students as a group to come up with an event to serve as a scene.

2. Ask each student to take on the voice of one of the people involved in this event and to write from that person's point of view.

3. You can further develop this as a lesson in theater by asking students to remain in character while others ask questions about their motivation and emotional response to the situation.

4. Alternatively, ask students to write a monologue in the voice of their favorite character from a book, television program, or movie.

Further Reading

Clifton, Lucille. *Blessing the Boats: New and Selected Poems 1988–2000*. Rochester, N.Y.: Boa Editions, 2000.

Garrison, Peggy. "Two Strings, One Pierced Cry: Writing Poems from Two Points of View Using Rita Dove's Poetry." In Lorenzo Thomas (ed.), *Sing the Sun Up: Creative Writing Ideas from African American Literature*. New York: Teachers & Writers Collaborative, 1998.

Hughes, Langston. "From Mother to Son." In Arnold Rampersad and David Roessel (ed.), *The Collected Poems of Langston Hughes*. New York: Vintage Books, 1995.

Ketchum, Liza. "Starting with Characters: Creating Written Portraits with Children." In Christopher Edgar and Ron Padgett (eds.), *Old Faithful: Eighteen Writers Present Their Favorite Writing Assignments*. New York: Teachers & Writers Collaborative, 1995.

Milosz, Czeslaw. "A Song on the End of the World." *The Collected Poems: 1931–1987*. New York: Ecco Press, 1988.

Paley, Grace. "Street Corner Dialogue." *New and Collected Poems*. Gardiner, Maine: Tillbury House, 1992.

Rodriguez, Luis. "Meeting the Animal in Washington Square Park." *Trochemoche*. Willimantic, Conn.: Curbstone Press, 1998.

Sirowitz, Hal. "Emergency Situation." *Mother Said: Poems*. New York: Crown Publishers, 1996.

Ziegler, Alan. "Writing About People." In Christopher Edgar and Ron Padgett (eds.), *Educating the Imagination: Essays and Ideas for Teachers and Writers*. New York: Teachers & Writers Collaborative, 2000.

Themes

When to Introduce Themes

As we've described, WritersCorps is a long-term, in-depth program. Our teachers share writing at their sites for a minimum of eight or nine months. In settings with  high participant turnover, a series of art attacks is often the best approach. In settings with a consistently attending group of students who share a relatively high level of trust, WritersCorps teachers often choose lessons that develop a theme and build on one another over time.

If your classroom provides such a setting, consider offering lessons that build into themes, thereby allowing students to examine a question from many angles or in increasing depth. Themes might relate to the literature that students are already reading in class (see "My Name is Esperanza" or the exercises under "Writing About Queer Identity" later in this chapter for examples). Perhaps your students are all recent immigrants or all queer-identified; such shared concerns allow for obvious themes. Your students might want to write about various aspects of the neighborhoods they live in. Or perhaps you'd like to suggest content that opens the door to greater personal exploration, such as writing about self and family.

Of course, writing about any of these themes may be painful. A youth may have buried early memories for a very

My song sounds
like the wind
blowing through
the trees
It looks and feels
velvet soft and
smooth as a petal
before it's plucked
or like sand falling
from my hands . . .

—Alegria Barclay,
WritersCorps teacher

good reason: family may be far away; a mother may have absconded; a father may be dead; a brother might be in prison; declaring one's sexual orientation is likely to be loaded with danger.

As always, please remember to tread softly, protect your students' privacy, and do all that's humanly possible to create emotional safety. As a teacher, of course, you try to be conscious and to assess the benefits and risks of any assignment. If you feel that a particular grouping of students is too volatile or if you're concerned about your own ability to respond to possible consequences, consider waiting for a less loaded moment to introduce potentially difficult material.

THE NATURE OF THEMES

You're likely to notice that many of the lessons in this chapter echo material we've offered as single exercises in other chapters. Students write about themselves in response to many of the exercises described in Chapter Four. Lessons in Chapter Five ask students to notice the world. Chapter Seven offers young writers opportunities to create stories—a form in which time expands from a single moment to past, present, and future. The difference is that in this chapter we're suggesting that you allow these single lessons to build on each other.

For example, one day you might ask the youth to write a poem based on the sound of their mother's voice. The next day you might suggest that students write about a gift from a family elder. The day after that, the writing exercise might ask for a story that the student's family has passed down, a description of the writer's hometown, or a repeated line that makes use of a parental injunction. These exercises could work alone, but taken lesson after lesson, each builds on what came before, creating a theme.

WRITING ABOUT YOURSELF

Exercise *Thirteen Ways of Looking at a Blackbird*

1. Read Wallace Stevens's poem "Thirteen Ways of Looking at a Blackbird."

2. Ask students to write a poem entitled "Thirteen Ways of Looking at Myself/My Life," using Stevens's poem as a model.

My Name Is Esperanza

1. Read the story about Esperanza's name from *The House on Mango Street,* a novel by Sandra Cisneros, or the following model poems. Point out the use of images in these poems.

My Name

My name is Tsz Wai
My name is like a trumpet
The sound passes through it
The sound is strong
My name is like a president
The fame spread to the whole earth
My name is like a sun
The shine can warm
Somebody wants to close it
Nobody can touch it
My name is like a sea
It's deep and wide
It's cool and blue
Some ships sink into it
If it gets lost
The earth will destroy.

Tsz Wai Chau

My Name Is February

My name is February
I stood beside a hill
Smooth with new-laid snow
A lonely star looked out from the distant dark evening sky
There was not another creature
I stood and watched the evening star
as long as it watched me

My name is like rarity
like a special sculpture that
nobody sees, and never
heard of for this fantastic rarity.

Aderito Sobral

2. Ask students to think about their own names. Ask them: Who named you? Why did they give you that name? Do you know what your name means? Do you have a different name at school or on the street than at home? What sounds do the letters of your name make—hard or soft, sharp or wavy? What similes and metaphors can you think of for these sounds? If you imagined a story for your name, what would that story be?

3. Ask students to write a poem or story about their names.

Exercise *When Other People Call My Name*

1. Ask students to think of five people in their lives who say their names often. Ask them to write what their names sound like when each of these people says it. Encourage them to include at least one person whom they don't particularly like. Here's an example.

My Name

When my sister says my name, it sounds like come here, I need you for something.

When Sandy says my name, it sounds like hello.

When Priscilla says my name, it sounds like did you see that thing on TV last night?

When Terry says my name, it sounds like can you come with me somewhere?

When my teachers say my name, it sounds dumb, not right.

Jennifer Brue, age thirteen

Exercise On the Day I Was Born

WritersCorps teacher Kim Nelson reports something that a linguist told her own teacher, playwright and actor Anna Deavere Smith. The linguist said that if you want the formal constructs to fall from a person's language so that natural speech emerges, ask the following three questions: Do you know anything about the circumstances of your birth? Have you ever had a brush with death? Have you ever been the recipient of injustice?

Kim chooses the first of these questions. You might create lessons that emphasize the other inquiries as well.

1. Ask students to make notes about everything they've heard about their birth. Prompts, if needed, include:

   Where were you born (hospital, home, city, state, country)?

   When were you born (month, day, time of day or night)?

   What is your astrological sign?

   Who named you?

   Do you have brothers and sisters?

   Are you the oldest child, the middle, the baby?

   Do you know what the weather was like when you were born?

2. Ask students to use their notes to write a poem about coming into this world.

Exercise Earliest Memories

1. Ask students to remember their earliest memories and to write about them.

2. Here are some questions to help students remember:

   What's a song you remember hearing on the radio or television or a song someone sang to you?

   Is it in your mother's or father's voice?

   Is a brother or sister talking to you or playing with you?

Do you remember your first, second, or third birthday party?

Do you remember any toys you had as a baby or toddler?

What's the first toy you remember?

Do you remember the house, apartment, or room where you lived?

Do you remember any walks in your stroller?

Exercise *If I Were an Animal*

1. Give students a handout you've prepared with these questions:

   What kind of animal are you?

   Where do you live?

   What do you dream about?

   What do you do?

2. Ask them to write a poem about this animal, using their answers to the handout questions.

Exercise *Tree of Life*

1. Ask your students to draw a tree.

2. Tell them that the trunk stands for their essential self; the roots are their strengths and beliefs, the things that hold them up; the branches, with their leaves and fruit, represent dreams and goals.

3. Ask students to write words on their tree to describe these aspects of themselves.

4. Ask them to write a poem or story based on these words.

Exercise *In My Room*

1. Share the book *My Room: Teenagers in Their Bedrooms* by Adrienne Salingers, which talks about and depicts teenagers in their bedrooms.

2. Ask students to write a piece called "In My Room."

Exercise Write About the Inner Self

1. Ask students to read and discuss the following model poem.

Incognito

I think 90 percent of me is Darkness.
The other 10 percent of me is good, pure, and clear as crystal.
I have lived in seclusion for so long, I can't relate
to people long enough to love them.
So I keep my distance.
I cannot predict the future, only live in the present
and watch the clock tick and stay tucked in the Dark.

Cleavon, age seventeen

2. Ask students to let this poem inspire them to write one of their own.

Exercise Cause and Effect

1. Read aloud the poem "Cause and Effect" by Peter Spiro. WritersCorps teacher Beto Palomar, who developed this lesson, points out that this poem presents a stark chain of events in a poor person's life, beginning with poor education and leading to prison and violent death.

2. Ask students to identify the poem's theme or message.

3. Ask students why they think the poet wrote this poem. Beto asks his students whether they agree that poor education can be a cause of a person's descent toward violence and crime. What are other causes that they see in their own lives, events, people, and conditions that they feel lead them down a particular path?

4. Ask students if they feel that the path of the person in the poem was inevitable. Do they feel that certain causes and effects in life are set and inevitable? How much power over our lives do we have? How much real choice?

5. Suggest that students write their own poem about a chain of events. For example: " 'cause you go to prison your life is wasted, 'cause your life is wasted

you are angry." Ask students to repeat the " 'cause you . . . , . . . occurs" form until they reach a conclusion.

Here is one student's poem to use as a model.

Cause and Effect

Cause you were listening to loud music
You didn't hear your mother call you
Cause you didn't hear your mother call you
Your mother turned off the stereo
Cause your mother turned off the stereo
You yelled at her with contempt
Cause you yelled at her with contempt
Your mother punished you
Cause your mother punished you
You became angry
Cause you became angry
You ran out of the home
Cause you ran out of the home
You didn't check the cars while
You crossed the avenue
Cause you didn't check the cars while you
Crossed the avenue
You were hit by a car
And you died.
Cause you were hit by a car
Cause you didn't check the cars while you
Crossed the avenue
Cause you ran out of the home
Cause you became angry
Cause your mother punished you
Cause you yelled at her with contempt
Cause your mother turned off the stereo
Cause you didn't hear your mother call you
Cause you were listening to loud music.

Jorge Aburto, age sixteen

I Live in a Doorway

1. WritersCorps teacher Mahru Elahi, who developed this lesson, reads and discusses the model poem below or Pat Mora's poem "*Sonrisas*" with her students.

2. Ask students to discuss or write quick responses to the following questions:

   What worlds are you a part of? (These could be racial, age, class, sexuality, gender, culture, language, work, and so on.)

   What worlds do you belong to but also feel you are sometimes outside of?

   What do these worlds look, sound, feel, taste, and smell like?

3. Ask students to write a poem in which the first stanza begins with the lines, "I live in a doorway / between two rooms, I hear . . ." and the second stanza begins, "I peek / in the other room . . ." Please allow students to experiment with other forms, should they so choose.

I Live

I live in a doorway between two rooms.
I hear a bunch of people acting up,
yelling and laughing.
Folks walking in and out of school,
always up to no good.
As I pass people by in the hallways I could smell
an ugly stench of rolled up blunts,
ready to be smoked
Walking by putting up fake smiles, hiding
what you really feel inside.

I peek in the other room meaningful
laughter.
Old stories being told of unforgettable
memories.
Finally being able to speak.

Maria Villalobos, age sixteen

Exercise *I Believe*

1. Ask students to talk about what they believe in—not just their political beliefs but their beliefs in and about all kinds of things. Do they believe in having best friends? In eating chocolate cake? Do they believe aliens once landed in New Mexico?

2. Ask students to write a poem about their beliefs after the group discussion. Let students know that they can also write about what they don't believe in: Santa, violence, drugs, and so on.

What I Believe

I still believe there are no heroes
   there is no real laughter
   there is anger hidden inside her heart
   there is a shadow in the corner, waiting to bite my ankle

I still believe in the nuclear threat
   we all bleed red
   Jesus is just dead
   I've made up everything in my head

I still believe that I can fly
   that I have wings
   that soar through the sky
   that let me believe

I still believe in peace
   in hope
   in love
   nobody believes in me

I still believe my mom loves me
   I am unique
   I can change the world
   I can make it on my own

I still believe that I can do anything with anything
   that there is another world out there somewhere
   that when you look into the sky
   there are people looking down upon us

I still believe
I still believe there is a devil underneath us looking up at us
I still believe.

    Anonymous

Exercise
My Song Is. .

1. Hand out a piece of paper with the following phrases and blank spaces:

   My song sounds like . . .

   My song looks and feels like . . .

   My song dreams about . . .

   My song dances and moves like . . .

   My song is as . . . as . . .

2. Read aloud the following poem by WritersCorps teacher Alegria Barclay, based on this structure.

My Song

My song sounds like the wind blowing through the trees
It looks and feels velvet soft and smooth as a petal before it's plucked
or like sand falling from my hands
My song dreams about days hot like an oven fire
nights warm as honey sliding down my throat
My song moves like great white clouds
gliding lazy across the sky
and dances like waves hurrying toward the shore
My song is as loud as an airplane's engine
flying far far away to my homeland
and leaving me behind.

3. Point out to the students that Alegria uses images. (If you wish, you can point out that these images are similes. You might ask how the feel of Alegria's poem would change if she'd used metaphors.) Alegria did not merely say "hot"; she wrote "hot like an oven fire." She did not write "warm" but "warm as honey sliding down my throat."

4. What other actions of waves might one compare her song to (crashing, retreating from the shore, and so forth)? Might Alegria have used other loud sounds as a comparison for her song's volume? What does the sound of an airplane engine add to the poem?

5. After discussing the model poem, ask students to write poems about the songs of their souls.

Exercise *Heart's Song*

1. Ask students to write a poem in which they say what is most important to them. A good model poem is "Heartsong" by Khaled Mattawa.

2. WritersCorps teacher Kim Nelson encourages students by saying, "Imagine you climbed to the roof of some building. Imagine it was just you and the sky and the stars or the sun and the buildings or trees, and you looked all around you and said what you have to say to the world. What would you say? Tell your heart's song."

3. Alternatively, you can ask students to pretend they have just one more hour to live: "What would you say in your last poem?"

Exercise *Write a Life Poem*

1. Give students a handout containing the following prompts:

My life is worth . . .

More than . . .

More than . . .

Because I am . . .

My life (feels like) . . .

I struggle against/with . . .

My life sounds like . . .

I dream about . . .

My life is as . . . as . . .

My life is worth . . .

2. Read the following model poem by a WritersCorps student.

My Life

My life is worth a plentiful feast that has gone untouched
More than a glutton's want of food
More than a warmonger's thirst for violence
More than the selfish man's quest for material things

Because I am myself and I'll be who and whatever I want to be
My life feels like an endless hallway of disappointment
I struggle with my inner self and forces I cannot control
My life sounds like the feeble heartbeat of a dying being
and my dreams of being with all whom I love
forever seems like a cruel trick
Each time I think I'm getting closer to the carrot
it just gets pulled further back
My life is as sweet as a rotting peach.

Jacqueline Wong, age seventeen

3. Ask students to write a poem from the list they have generated to complete the list of prompts in step one of this exercise.

Exercise *Amnesia Strikes*

1. Tell students that in fifteen minutes they will lose all memories and images from their past. (Some teachers like to pretend that the memory police or aliens are arriving and will confiscate all the students' memories.)

2. Ask students to write down as many memories as possible in the fifteen-minute period so as not to lose them forever.

3. Ask students to pick one memory and write a poem or story about it.

Exercise Mix Up Memories, Mix Up Lines

1. Ask students to think of one of their earliest childhood memories.

2. Ask them to write five sentences about this memory, each on a separate line.

3. Ask students to remember a vivid dream or nightmare and to write five sentences about this dream on five separate lines.

4. Ask students to cut apart all the sentences and rearrange the resulting ten lines.

5. Ask students to copy these lines in the arrangement they like into their journals or on a separate sheet of paper.

6. Then ask everyone to place their sentences in the middle of the table or on the floor. Mix these up.

7. Ask each student to take a handful of sentences, arrange them, and copy them onto paper.

Exercise Pick a Number

1. Write different numbers from one to one hundred on scraps of paper.

2. Ask students to choose one of these pieces of paper and then write about themselves when they were that age or when they will be that age.

Exercise Pick a Color

1. Bring in paper or fabric of various colors.

2. Ask students to select one swatch (or have them choose one at random). Ask students to write about the meaning of this color in their lives.

Here is a model poem by a WritersCorps student.

Kalu

Black is Anthony, the person who is talking now.
Black is beautiful, like everyone here.
Black is a color that no one understands.

Black is cold like when you shiver in the snow.

Black is someone like you and me.

Black can fly like a bird in the sky.

Black is shiny like the sun upon us.

Black is a flower.

Black is Anthony, the one who finished the poem.

Anthony Miller, age twelve

WRITING ABOUT FAMILY

Exercise *Memories of Relatives*

1. Ask students to write the words *name* and *relationship* at the top of a sheet of paper.

2. Ask them to list all family members, putting first and last names in the name column and each member's relationship to the student in the relationship column.

3. Ask them to choose one relative and write either their first or last memory of this person. It doesn't matter if the incident happened in person, on the phone, or through a letter. They can write a poem, a story, or a remembrance or memoir.

4. Ask each student to read at least part of what she wrote.

Exercise *Write About Family Photographs*

1. Ask students to bring family photographs to class.

2. Write a poem or a story based on these photos.

Exercise *Grandparents and Ancestors*

1. Read model poems that you've found (in your own reading or elsewhere in *Jump Write In!*) about grandmothers, grandfathers, and ancestors.

2. Because you're going to ask your students for personal details, talk about your own grandparents. What names did you call them? Did you know them well? What were the stories you heard about them?

3. Ask students what they call (or used to call) their grandparents. Ask them to use their senses to evoke the smells, tastes, foods, and games that they associate with their grandparents.

4. Then ask them to write a poem using these memories.

Exercise The Community as Family

1. Ask students to make a list (either individually or by brainstorming as a group) of questions about family and community that they can ask each other or someone outside the class.

2. Prompt students by asking them to think about these questions:

   Where are you from, and have you lived there your entire life?

   What makes up a family?

   What does a family feel like?

   Who are you close to and why?

   What funny memories do you have of your family?

   How do you define community?

3. Ask students to write five questions that they can use for interviews about family and community.

4. Ask students to interview each other and one person outside class. They will then write up the results of these interviews.

WRITING ABOUT HOLIDAYS

Writing about the holidays can be a mixed blessing for many WritersCorps students, who may be separated from their families or living in unhappy families.

When working with students for whom holidays bring up pain and loss, you might offer hands-on activities such as making cards. For Thanksgiving at Log Cabin Ranch, where students are incarcerated, teacher Kim Nelson brings in chips and soda rather than traditional Thanksgiving fare and asks everyone to say one thing he's thankful for. Kim also brings in poems about the difficulties that can arise over the holidays and shares these with her students.

The exercises that follow deal with only a handful of holidays. Ask your students about the holidays that matter to them and try to develop relevant writing exercises based on those special dates (for example, Cesar Chavez's birthday, Kwanzaa, Ramadan, and so forth).

Exercise **Look Back on the Year**

1. Have the students say good-bye to the current year before New Year's Day.

2. Prepare a handout with the following or similar prompts:

   If last year were a person, it would be . . .

   If last year were a car, it would be . . .

   If last year were a drink, it would taste like . . .

   If last year were music, it would sound like . . .

   If last year were an animal, it would be . . .

   If last year were a piece of clothing, it would be . . .

   If last year were a kind of weather, it would be . . .

   If last year were a color, it would be . . .

3. Ask students to write a poem about the year that is ending.

Exercise **Poems to the New Year**

1. Pass out a sheet of paper that presents the following form from which students can write a poem for the new year:

   This new year I want to see . . .

   I want to see . . .

   I want to see . . .

   I don't want to see . . .

   This new year I want to hear . . .

I want to hear . . .

I want to hear . . .

I don't want to hear . . .

This new year I want to touch . . .

I want to touch . . .

I want to touch . . .

I don't want to touch . . .

This new year I want to smell . . .

I want to smell . . .

I want to smell . . .

I don't want to smell . . .

This new year I want to taste . . .

I want to taste . . .

I want to taste . . .

I don't want to taste . . .

2. You might use this form to remind students that imagery in poems employs material from all five senses.

Exercise
Chinese New Year

1. At Chinese New Year, talk about the Chinese calendar and its signs, giving students information about the characteristics of the animal sign under which they were born.

2. Ask students to write a poem or story about their future, making use of the information they learn about their Chinese animal sign.

Exercise
Valentine's Day

1. Brainstorm about different kinds of love: platonic, romantic, and so on.

2. Ask students to write a poem about a form of love other than romantic. Students might enjoy writing antivalentines. Of course, if you open this door,

please be sure to reinforce previously established expectations about mutual respect and group safety.

Exercise
Martin Luther King Jr. and the Civil Rights Movement

Every year WritersCorps honors the work and memory of the Reverend Martin Luther King Jr. by sponsoring a poetry contest in his honor. WritersCorps teachers ask students to write poems about the principles of civil rights and freedom. The winning poem is printed and distributed in San Francisco on Martin Luther King Jr. Day in January.

The subject matter is rich with possibilities. Here is an opportunity for teachers to talk not only about Martin Luther King Jr. but also about the civil rights movement, race relations, the qualities of a leader, heroes, and so on.

1. Bring in photographs from the days of segregation, such as of a water fountain with a "whites only" sign or a bus with whites in the front rows and blacks in the back rows.

2. Ask students to imagine living in a world with such overt racism and then write a poem about how the times have changed or not changed since Martin Luther King Jr.'s death.

Here's the winning poem from the year 2000.

Work for Change

for the Reverend Martin Luther King Jr.
You worked for people of color,
died for your great work.
We will remember you forever.
Now people of color have more power than before.
"Whites Only" sign,
no longer on the restaurant's door.
We can sit in any seat on the bus.
Even the mayor of San Francisco is not a white man.

Of course there is not total equality.
The white people and the rich
may look down on the colored and poor.
The United States has changed but still is unfair.
People from other countries do not
have as much power as people born here.
We have a lot of work to do to make all people equal.

Penelope Zheng, age seventeen

WRITING ABOUT YOUR NEIGHBORHOOD

Exercise *What I Smell, See, Touch*

Many WritersCorps teachers have found Francisco X. Alarcón's poem "The Mission" (in English and Spanish) an excellent model poem for this exercise.

1. Ask students to describe their neighborhoods in detail.

2. They can write about the neighborhood as a whole or about a specific street, a street corner, or a favorite hangout.

3. Remind students to recall sensory information: What do they see, hear, smell, taste, and touch?

Exercise *Build a Monument*

1. Take a field trip to a particular place where you live (WritersCorps teachers in San Francisco have taken their students to sites such as Coit Tower, Golden Gate Park, Market Street, and so on).

2. Ask students to become city planners and to design their own monument (it could also be a park, bridge, or building). Whom would they honor? What would they have on the monument?

Students working with WritersCorps teacher Elizabeth Meyer constructed what they called Tenderloin Towers after looking at material about the Watts Tower in Los Angeles. They used clay, wire, and found objects as their building materials.

3. Ask students to write a story or poem about the monument they built.

Exercise *City of Dreams*

1. Take your students on a tour of your city (for example, in San Francisco: Golden Gate Park, the Financial District, Mission District, Hyde Street Pier).

2. Bring in art materials and ask students to build a model of their city of dreams. Would the city have parks, public transportation, theaters, libraries, and so forth?

3. Ask students to write a poem or story about their ideal city.

Exercise *Do Not Enter*

1. Ask students to write a poem that uses a street sign as its title or theme. For example: "Do Not Enter," "Yield," "Stop," "Dead End," "Speed Limit," or "One Way."

2. Prompt students by asking: What does this sign mean in your life? Who would say these words to you and why? Are you telling someone to stop or that there is only one way? Would you obey your sign—not just in driving but in living your life?

REMEMBERING A HOMELAND

Exercise *Here and There*

1. In a classroom in which most students have come from elsewhere, ask youth to brainstorm about the components of culture and country: food, holidays, music, religion, dress, animals, weather, and so on. What makes living in one place different from living in another? Write responses on the chalkboard or on chart paper.

2. Divide students into groups of four or five.

3. Have each group pick three of the cultural components you've listed (for instance, language, food, and holidays) and create a chart by writing the components on a large piece of paper.

4. Ask students to fill in the chart by writing their name, country of origin, and the selected cultural components from their respective countries. Of course,

some students may be native North Americans, in which case the United States will be their country of origin. Or perhaps you might suggest that these students choose a particular city or state they've come from to identify as home.

Here's a sample chart:

Name	Country	Language	Food	Holiday
Eduardo	Philippines	Tagalog	lumpia	Christmas
Raul	Mexico	Spanish	mango	Día de los Muertos
Sheila	China	Cantonese	rice	Chinese New Year

5. Ask each group to present its chart to the whole class or workshop.

Ask students to write poems individually, using details from their countries of origin and details from the United States as a whole or the city where they live now. If you wish, you can provide students with a prompt, such as "I remember . . ."; "In my country . . . but here"; or "I am glad to be here because . . . , but I am sad because . . ."

Here's a student example.

I Remember the Philippines

I remember when I was in my beloved country, peaceful and listening
    to birds' songs.
I remember playing in the front yard of the house with friends.
I remember our games we played, hide and seek, gathering flowers to
    make decorations.
I remember that our yards were planted with different flowers and
fruit trees: guava, *goyavano,* star apple, mango, and banana.
I remember eating fresh fruits that were newly harvested from the tree.
In my country we had our own house to live in and yard to play in.
But here we rent our house and there's no yard to play in.
In my country every day I could hear birds singing sweetly in the tree.
But here there are no trees and no birds to sing.
In my country we have tree fruits to harvest, fresh fruits.
But here we have to buy it in a store, not fresh.
In my country we have a lot of beautiful plants that we could take care of.

But here we don't have plants, only just the hanging plants.
In my country it is peaceful with fresh air.
But here it is crowded, polluted air, and noisy.

I am sad because I'm not in my country to enjoy again the living I got
    used to
And to live again like it was before.
And I still remember . . .

Susana Mostoles, age seventeen

Exercise *The Border*

This exercise also is appropriate for a classroom in which most students have come from elsewhere.

1. Ask students to draw up two lists. The first list is a series of words indicating things they left behind in their countries (or cities or states) of origin (for example, people, things, places, and animals). The second list is a series of words indicating what they have found in this country.

2. Ask students to think about the "borders" that separate these two places: the actual borders, rivers, resources necessary to pay for airfare, history, choices, and so on.

3. Ask them to write a poem that incorporates as many words as possible from both lists.

Exercise *Interview Your Homeland*

Here is another exercise for immigrants, building on the theme of homeland and new land.

1. Ask students to "interview" their native countries and to have the country answer the questions. You might begin with a brainstorm session in which students think of questions to ask. Note that this exercise uses personification.

2. Encourage students to write the piece in their native tongue as well as in English and to use the dialogue form.

Exercise *Looking for America*

This exercise is appropriate for a classroom of both newcomers and students whose families have lived in the United States for generations.

1. Read out loud Janice Mirikitani's poem "Looking for America."

2. Discuss what the speaker of the poem was looking for, what she found, and where she found it.

3. Ask about the images in the poem, the repeated stereotypes, and the illusions.

4. Ask students to look for themselves in America. Where do they see images of themselves in this country (television, magazines, movies, and so on)? What are those images? If you wish, you can ask additional questions, such as: Who tries to create images of you? What are these images? Who tries to speak for you? What do they say for you? Where do you really see yourself?

5. Ask them to make a list of these words and images.

6. Then ask students to write a poem that reflects their own experience of searching for images of themselves. You might suggest that they use the lines Mirikitani uses to start the three stanzas of her poem: "I searched for my-self"; "I found myself"; "I meet myself."

Exercise *Visit Your Homeland*

1. Ask students to "visit" their native countries (even if their families arrived on North American soil generations ago) using their imagination.

2. Share photographic images from these countries and ask students what they notice. What's the weather? What kinds of crops grow in that country? What kinds of clothes do people wear? Bring up as much historical and cultural information as you wish.

3. Write a poem or story about the visit.

WritersCorps teacher Alegria Barclay took her students to visit Vietnam, the country her mother came from. She also made the exercise into a game by having students board an imaginary plane and fly to Vietnam.

Exercise: Translate Poems

1. Ask students whose first language is not English to translate a poem from their native languages into their new tongue.

2. Alternatively, they can translate a poem in English into their native languages.

WRITING ABOUT QUEER IDENTITY

In 1996 WritersCorps teacher Ellis Avery created two four-week sessions on writing about queer identity, which she offered to students at Lavender Youth Recreation and Information Center (LYRIC)—a WritersCorps site in San Francisco. LYRIC serves queer youth, so Ellis developed these exercises for a specific population who had chosen to meet together.

To use this material with a mixed group, one in which some youth are straight and some may be homophobic, you will have to adapt these lessons. We present them as Ellis created them because of their inherent value and also as an example of how to develop a theme when working with a group of youth sharing a specific concern or history.

Telling Our Stories Our Way

Ellis designed the first four-week course, "Live It Your Own Way," to encourage students to tell each other their stories. With that practice, Ellis says, "We can decide what we want to tell curious straight people and what we want to hold on to for ourselves."

The four weeks of "Live It Your Own Way" focus first on the ancestral past, then the personal past, the present, and the future.

Exercise: Remembering Our Ancestral Past

Choose one or more of the following prompts as a catalyst for writing:

1. Poet and novelist Cherríe Moraga's line "I am the queer memory of my family."

2. Dorothy Allison's novel *Bastard Out of Carolina:* ask students to write about a secret or confession that a family member told them.

3. Poet Sapphire's novel *Push:* ask students to create a myth using their own life stories and experiences.

4. After a student has read what he or she has written, ask the others to repeat what they remember from the piece. This validates the writer's work and helps him discover the catchiest or most memorable aspects of his poem, story, or essay.

Exercise Remembering Our Past

Choose one or more of the following prompts as a catalyst for writing:

1. Ask students to freewrite for five minutes, beginning with the prompt "I remember."

2. Ask students to describe who they fantasized about as a child, starting with the line "Now I am a girl [or boy], but one day I will marry a woman [or man]" from Jamaica Kincaid's story "In the Night."

3. Ask students to write their first memories of hearing or using the words *gay, lesbian, queer,* and so on.

4. Ask students to write about the first time they realized that they were gay and that some people (perhaps their parents) didn't want them to be gay.

Exercise Write About the Present

Choose one or more of the following prompts as a catalyst for writing:

1. Ask students to freewrite for five minutes, repeating the line "The place where I live is . . ." over and over.

2. Ask students to think about where they feel most comfortable and where they don't feel they belong.

3. Ask students to write about these places.

Exercise Write About What the Future Holds

1. Ask students to freewrite for five minutes, repeating the line "In my tomorrow."

2. Ask students to write about their images of their futures.

Fierce and Real: Celebrating Honesty

Ellis called the second four-week course "Fierce and Real." This workshop's goal was to explore the damage caused by lying about one's sexual orientation and, as Ellis says, to "celebrate the deeply restorative power of being honest about who we are and who we love."

Exercise *Lies I've Told*

Choose one or more of the following prompts as a catalyst for writing:

1. Ask students to freewrite for five minutes, repeating the line "I never told you . . ." or "I didn't tell you . . ." If it seems appropriate, ask them to follow this line with "Instead, I said . . ."

2. Ask students to write about a time that they lied to their families through words or actions.

3. Ask students to write about a time that they lied by not speaking up or by pretending not to see something.

4. Ask students to write about a time that they helped someone lie or that someone helped them lie.

Exercise *Lying to Myself*

Choose one or more of the following prompts as a catalyst for writing:

1. Ask students to freewrite for five minutes, repeating the line "I didn't want to believe . . . " or "I didn't want to know . . ."

2. Ask students to write about how it feels to lie to oneself. Ask them to compare this feeling to something else—a color, an object, and so forth. Ellis used excerpts from Toni Morrison's novel *Sula* as a model.

3. Read "Linoleum Roses," a chapter from *The House on Mango Street,* the novel by Sandra Cisneros. Ask students to write about a time when they watched a person lie to herself.

4. Ask students to write about a time when a friend called them on lying to themselves. How did they react?

Exercise *Telling the Truth to Myself*

Choose one or more of the following prompts as a catalyst for writing:

1. Ask students to freewrite for five minutes, repeating the line "Now I know . . ." several times.

2. Ask students to write about a time when they knew that acknowledging their desires was more important than what other people thought about them.

3. Ask students to write about a time when they knew their truth but could not articulate it to others.

Exercise *Speaking Up*

1. Ask students to freewrite for five minutes, repeating the line "I spoke up and said . . ."

2. If it feels appropriate, ask students to write about a time when they came out to someone. Whom did they tell? How did they feel? Were they scared? Were they full of hope?

Further Reading

Alarcón, Francisco X. "The Mission." *Body in Flames/Cuerpo en Llamas.* San Francisco: Chronicle Books, 1990.

Allison, Dorothy. *Bastard Out of Carolina.* New York: Plume, 1993.

Cisneros, Sandra. *The House on Mango Street.* New York: Vintage Contemporaries, 1991.

Goldfarb, Sidney. "Archaeology of the City." In Ron Padgett and Bill Zavatsky (eds.), *The Whole Word Catalogue 2.* New York: Teachers & Writers Collaborative, 1987.

Kincaid, Jamaica. "In the Night." *At the Bottom of the River.* New York: Farrar, Straus and Giroux, 1978.

King, Casey, and Osborne, Linda Barrett (eds.). *Oh Freedom: Kids Talk About the Civil Rights Movement with the People Who Made It Happen.* New York: Knopf, 1997.

King, Dr. Martin Luther, Jr. "Letter from the Birmingham Jail." In David J. Garrow (ed.), *Eyes on the Prize Civil Rights Reader: Documents, Speeches, and Firsthand Accounts from the Black Freedom Struggle, 1954–1990.* New York: Penguin, 1991.

Mattawa, Khaled. "Heartsong." In *Best American Poetry.* New York: Scribner, 1997.

Mirikitani, Janice. "Looking for America." *We, the Dangerous: New and Selected Poems.* Berkeley: Ten Speed Press, 1996.

Mora, Pat. "Sonrisas." In Laurie R. King (ed.), *Hear My Voice: A Multicultural Anthology of Literature from the United States.* New York: Addison-Wesley, 1993.

Moraga, Cherrie. *Last Generation: Prose and Poetry.* Boston: South End Press, 1993.

Morrison, Toni. *Sula.* New York: New American Library, 1989.

Neruda, Pablo. *Book of Questions.* Port Townsend, Wash.: Copper Canyon Press, 1991.

Salingers, Adrienne. *My Room: Teenagers in Their Bedrooms.* San Francisco: Chronicle Books, 1995.

Saltzman, Suzann Steele. "Writing Vignettes with Sandra Cisneros's House on Mango Street." In Julio Marzan (ed.), *Luna, Luna: Creative Writing Ideas from Spanish, Latin American, and Latino Literature.* New York: Teachers & Writers Collaborative, 1997.

Sapphire. *Push.* New York: Vintage Books, 1997.

Spiro, Peter. "Cause and Effect." In Miguel Algarín and Bob Holman (eds.), *Aloud: Voices from the Nuyorican Poets Café.* New York: Henry Holt and Company, 1994.

Stevens, Wallace. "Thirteen Ways of Looking at a Blackbird." *The Collected Poems of Wallace Stevens.* New York: Vintage, 1990.

Washington, James Melvin (ed.). *A Testament of Hope: The Essential Writings of Martin Luther King.* San Francisco: Harper, 1991.

Writing with Visual Art

**I will use my hands
to disperse
the darkness
in the sky
I want to see the
whole moon. . . .
I want to see the
sky clearly.**

—Francisco

Art Inspires Writing

Even on days when your students are too tired, too agitated, or too distracted to write, often they are in the mood to draw or do an art project. As we suggested in this book's introduction, make drawing materials easily available in your classroom and occasionally offer unusual surfaces on which students can write. WritersCorps teachers in San Francisco go to SCRAP or the East Bay Depot for Creative Re-Use to find art supplies and found objects that students can use in art projects or as triggers for writing. Look for similar recycling centers in your community.

If field trips are a possibility, consider taking your students to a museum, gallery, or public art installation. Ask the youth

NCTE/IRA Standards
Standards 1– 7; 10–12

to write poems or stories inspired by the artwork—preferably right at the site or later when you return to your classroom.

YOUNGER CHILDREN

Although *Jump Write In!* shares lessons appropriate for students of middle and high school age, WritersCorps teachers adapt many of these ideas for use with younger children. You can do the same. Projects that combine art and writing especially lend themselves to work with elementary-age youngsters.

DRAWING AND DICTATION

Some children are either too young or simply not ready to write. In those cases, having them draw a picture while they dictate their story or poem to you might be more effective. You can write their words on the same sheet that contains their drawing.

DRAWING AS A PROMPT

Exercise *Hand Poems*

1. Ask students to trace their hands with colored markers.
2. Share model poems with students. For example, read Naomi Shihab Nye's poem "Daily" or the following model poem by a WritersCorps student.

My Hands

I will use my hands to disperse
the darkness in the sky
I want to see the whole
moon.
"Hands,
remove the clouds now.
I want to see the sky clearly."

Francisco

3. Ask students to fill in the outlines of their hands with a poem that describes what their hands can do. Encourage students to use as much concrete description as possible.

Exercise Body Portraits

Feel free to bring out all the craft materials you've gathered to decorate this one: glitter, fluorescent paper, buttons, glue, and so on.

1. Ask students to pair up and trace their partner's outline on butcher paper.

2. Ask students to write on the silhouettes: their dreams on the head, their feelings where their hearts are, and their destination on their feet.

3. Ask students to use these body portraits as the basis for writing a poem or story about themselves.

Exercise Visit to Another Planet

WritersCorps teacher Alison Seevak developed this exercise with a group of six- to nine-year-olds.

1. Read aloud *Fat Men in Space* by Daniel Pinkwater.

2. Ask students to draw their own planets to visit.

3. While they're drawing, ask them to show you what the creatures on that planet look like. What do they eat? Where do they live? What do they wear? Ask students to give their planets and creatures names.

4. When students finish drawing, have each one dictate a story about the world they've created as you write their words on the drawing. Alternatively, you can let them write their stories on the drawings.

SELF-PORTRAITS

Exercise *Mirror, Mirror*

1. Bring a hand mirror for each student.

2. Ask students to look at themselves and to draw self-portraits.

3. You can bring in examples of self-portraits to share. In addition to realistic work, bring in examples of fantastic, surreal, and comic-book-style self-portraits to show students the range of options.

4. Once they've finished drawing, ask students to write about their self-portraits.

5. Frame the self-portraits.

Exercise *Fortune-Tellers*

1. Ask students to look in hand mirrors and to draw themselves as they'll look in the future. Or they can draw their grandchildren or great-grandchildren.

2. Ask them to write fortunes for their futures.

Exercise *Photos as Self-Portraits*

You can do this exercise over the course of two or three separate sessions, assuming the same students show up to class each time. You will need a Polaroid or digital camera and film (or access to a computer).

1. During the first session, bring examples of photographers' portraits to illustrate that a portrait needn't be of a face. Share, for example, Alfred Stieglitz's portraits of Georgia O'Keefe's hands.

2. Ask students to think about how they would like to be represented in a portrait. What kind of pose do they want? Do they have a piece of clothing, an icon, a talisman, or a special piece of jewelry they want included? If so, ask them to bring this material to the next session.

3. During the second session, the students pair up and take Polaroid or digital photos of each other.

4. On the third day, read and look at the following photo-essay books edited by Jim Goldberg: *Raised by Wolves, Hospice: A Photographic Inquiry,* or *Rich and Poor.* These combine self-portraits with words.

5. Give each student a blank sheet of paper along with mounting corners, and ask them to place their picture in the corners.

6. Ask students to write words that go with their portraits. Encourage them by asking: What do you see in this photo? What do you want to tell people about yourself through this portrait? You can also use prompts such as these:

   I feel . . .

   This picture is about . . .

   This photo makes me want to . . .

   I am . . .

   My life is . . .

   I am trying . . .

   I look (like) . . .

   I wish . . .

   My dream is . . .

7. If you plan to gather these portraits into a book, make sure that students write in black pen or some other medium that will photocopy well.

MAPPING

We usually define the word *map* as a representation on a flat surface of an area. Though most often it represents a region such as a city or country, a map can be a surface on which we metaphorically map other aspects of ourselves and our experience, as in the following exercises.

Exercise **Map of My Body**

1. Ask students to draw a "map" of their bodies. One way to do this is to have them pair up and trace an outline of their partner's bodies. You can also interpret the word *map* less literally and have them draw the body in a more abstract or interpretive way.

2. Ask students to show on the drawing their bodies' histories through words and art. A student might draw his feet planted on one spot and his arms extended. This student might write, "My feet walk the hills of San Francisco, but my arms reach out to China, my homeland."

3. An excellent book to share with younger students as you do this exercise is *My Map Book* by Sara Fanelli. The book includes examples such as "Map of My Family," "Map of My Day," maps of tummies and faces, and so on.

Exercise **The Beautiful Country of Me**

1. Tell students that they are now queen or president or boss of their own countries. Ask them to name their country, decide how it's run, and determine the customs and values of their people.

2. Ask students to choose a physical position in which to be traced.

3. Trace the outlines of students' bodies on huge sheets of paper.

4. In this way each student makes a map of her country. As WritersCorps teacher Gloria Yamato, who designed this project when working with young girls at Girls After School Academy, says: "This exercise allows the girls' bodies to become countries that they alone preside over."

Exercise **Map of My Life**

1. Ask students to list the most memorable events of their lives and the geographical locations in which these events occurred.

2. Using either collage or freehand drawing, ask students to create a map of their lives.

3. Ask them to turn these maps into texts, using the prompt "My memory is like a map, and when I look at it I see . . ."

Exercise *Map of My Homeland*

1. Ask students to draw a map of the country or state where they were born and raised, the land that their parents and grandparents are from, or a place they're fond of. Have an atlas available to assist them.

2. Ask students to write at least thirty words that they associate with that country or state. Encourage them to record sensory details (sights, sounds, and smells).

3. Ask students to write a poem inside their map outlines that incorporates as many of their thirty words as possible.

Here are two examples by WritersCorps students.

Jamaica

I'm in Jamaica
eating goat &
fishballs &
listening to
music. People
by the dock &
people behind
buildings with
drums saying
good morning
good afternoon
and good night.

Sharina Weatherspoon, age eleven

Mexico

Mexico reminds me of my *tío's* fruit trees.

Mexico reminds me of hot sun burning the dirty streets.

Mexico reminds me of loud barking dogs, fat pigs, and chickens.

Mexico reminds me of donkeys and pretty black horses.

It reminds me of my cousins and all the time we spend talking when I visit.

Mexico reminds me of eating that spicy *menudo* with extra cow skin.

Mexico reminds me of the brown eagle in the center of the Mexican flag.

Alejandra Gamez, age fourteen

FAMILY TREE

Exercise *Trace Your Genealogy*

1. Introduce and discuss the history and function of genealogy and family trees.

2. Ask students to list the people in their family trees and to write an anecdote or personal association connected with each of these people.

3. Ask students to create a visual representation of this tree, incorporating the people and associations they've written.

COLLAGES

Exercise *Piece a Poem Together*

1. Ask each participant to cut out fifteen words (five nouns, five verbs, and five adjectives) from magazines you've brought in.

2. Ask students to arrange these words into a poem by gluing them onto a piece of paper.

3. Have students cut out images from the magazines to illustrate their words.

Exercise **The Billboard**

1. Ask students to imagine that they have artistic control of a billboard in a central location in your town.

2. Ask students to use clippings from newspapers, magazines, and postcards to design a personal message to the city.

Exercise **Word Borders**

1. Ask students to draw the outline of their country's or state's shape on a large piece of paper. You can bring in an atlas to help them. Tell them to leave room around the outline for the writing they will do after they have completed the collages.

2. Ask them to write phrases that describe their country (or state)—words that represent or paint a picture of the place—on the outline's border.

3. In the same class session or another session, bring magazines and ask students to fill their country's shape with a collage. Ask them to choose pictures that say something about who they are as individuals—their likes, dislikes, personalities, hobbies, and so on. Each student ends up with a finished collage bordered with words describing his country of origin.

4. Ask students to write couplets (paired lines of poetry) on their collages using the following structure:

   I (followed by a line derived from the pictures they've chosen to represent who they are on the collage)

   Name of their country (followed by a line that uses the words they've written around the border to describe their country)

5. If there is room, students can copy the couplets onto their collages.

Here are some examples.

I am a map
Ethiopia is rain.

Hiwot Wolday, age sixteen

I smell the night ocean
Bosnia smells war on her chest.

Sanjin Handan, age sixteen

I like every kind of music
Indonesia likes the rhyme of the sea.

Dianawaty Rahardjo, age fifteen

MORE ART-RELATED EXERCISES

Exercise Make Masks

1. Ask students to think of a time when they felt that they had to wear a mask. Perhaps it was when someone hurled a racial slur at them or when a relative or friend died and they did not want others to see their grief.

2. Have students make a mask out of scraps, construction paper, glue, and so forth.

3. Read model poems about masks. Some good ones are Paul Laurence Dunbar's "We Wear the Mask" and Maya Angelou's "Song for the Old Ones."

4. Ask students to write a story or poem in the mask's voice or about the mask and what it means to them.

Exercise Poetry Mobile

1. Ask students to write one of their poems on a sheet of colored construction paper and cut out the poem in any shape. They can tape or glue the shapes to make them three-dimensional.

2. Ask students to string all the poems onto mobiles, which you can hang in your classroom.

Exercise Comic Strips

1. Introduce the subject of comic strips and graphic novels, discussing the ways in which they tell a story in pictures.

2. Introduce some vocabulary associated with comics: panel, dialogue, monologue, thought clouds, and bubbles.

3. Ask students to share stories about their favorite superheroes.

4. Ask students to create their own comic strips.

Exercise Concrete Poetry

Concrete poems play with space on the page, typeface, symbols, colors, and sound to create a poem whose meaning is derived as much from how it looks as what the words actually mean. Because concrete poems are visual, they elevate the poem to a kind of graphic art.

1. Share examples of concrete poems, such as Apollinaire's "It's Raining" or John Hollander's "Swan and Shadow" and "Eskimo Pie."

2. Ask students to create their own concrete poems.

Exercise Picture Poems

Part of a tradition that includes medieval illuminated manuscripts, the engravings of William Blake, and concrete poetry, picture poems refer to the painted and collaged poems of twentieth-century poet Kenneth Patchen.

1. Share the picture poems of Kenneth Patchen (*What Shall We Do Without Us?*).

2. Ask students to create their own picture poems.

Exercise *Cancellation Poems*

1. Discuss the ways in which written language surrounds us every day (billboards, newspapers, advertisements, street signs, and so forth) and whether this kind of language is poetic.

2. Give students a sheet of paper with text from a newspaper article or words from a billboard, street sign, or advertisement.

3. Ask students to create a cancellation poem by crossing out words in the text.

Further Reading

Angelou, Maya. "Song for the Old Ones." *Oh Pray My Wings Are Gonna Fit Me Well.* New York: Random House, 1975.

Apollinaire. "It's Raining." In Milton Klonksy (ed.), *Speaking Pictures: A Gallery of Pictorial Poetry from the Sixteenth Century to the Present.* New York: Harmony Books, 1975.

Collom, Jack, and Noethe, Sheryl. *Poetry Everywhere.* New York: Teachers & Writers Collaborative, 1994.

Dunbar, Paul Laurence. "We Wear the Mask." *The Collected Poetry of Paul Laurence Dunbar.* Charlottesville: University of Virginia Press, 1993.

Fanelli, Sara. *My Map Book.* New York: HarperCollins Juvenile Books, 1995.

Galt, Margot Fortunato. "The Great Migration: Using the Art of Jacob Lawrence and the Poetry of Langston Hughes and Gwendolyn Brooks." In Lorenzo Thomas (ed.), *Sing the Sun Up: Creative Writing Ideas from African American Literature.* New York: Teachers & Writers Collaborative, 1998.

Goldberg, Jim. *Rich and Poor.* New York: Random House, 1985.

Goldberg, Jim. *Raised by Wolves.* Zurich: Scalo Books, 1995.

Goldberg, Jim. *Hospice: A Photographic Inquiry.* New York: Bulfinch Press, 1996.

Greenough, Sarah (ed.). *Alfred Stieglitz: The Key Set, Vol. I and II. The Alfred Stieglitz Photographs.* New York: Abrams, 2002.

Hollander, John. "Swan and Shadow" and "Eskimo Pie." In Milton Klonksy (ed.), *Speaking Pictures: A Gallery of Pictorial Poetry from the Sixteenth Century to the Present.* New York: Harmony Books, 1975.

Patchen, Kenneth. *What Shall We Do Without Us?* San Francisco: Sierra Club Books, 1984.

Pinkwater, Daniel. *Fat Men in Space.* New York: Yearling Books, 1980.

Shihab Nye, Naomi. "Daily." *Words Under the Words: Selected Poems.* Portland, Oreg.: Eighth Mountain Press, 1987.

Editing and Rewriting

The Importance of Revision

After ten chapters filled with ideas to inspire new writing, it's now time to turn to the editing of existing work. Beginning

writers often feel that a first draft is a final draft; the teacher's task is to share the process of revision as an integral part of the craft.

WritersCorps teacher Chad Sweeney suggests that students think of editing as writing a second draft. Correcting mistakes is only a small part of editing; the more exciting task is to find ways to enliven the writing, refresh worn-out phrases, and even begin working with new ideas that didn't come up in the first draft.

For example, WritersCorps teacher Hoa Nguyen was dissatisfied with the chant poems her students wrote. "The poems seemed, well, dull," she says. "I had the feeling after that session was over that they were merely pushing their pens across the page, doing the minimum to satisfy the exercise and me." Hoa decided to hold an editing session with her students.

Ask students to think about the activity of language.

NCTE/IRA Standards
Standards 1–6; 9–12

During that class she read the students' first drafts and asked these young writers to think about what she calls the "activity of the language." She shared examples of chants that she herself had written and handed out a worksheet to assist her students.

Hoa also asked the writers to come up with a phrase that they would repeat and to create two lists, one of verbs and another of adjectives and nouns. The students wrote these words on blank index cards, shuffled the cards, and then chose a couple to build lines from. Hoa also gave each student a few of her own word cards to vary their vocabulary. "On those I tried to provide kicky verbs and provocative adjectives," she says.

Here's an example of the results from this class. Student Linh Nguyen originally wrote:

The Willow Branch

The willow branch gives me luck
It will keep me safe
when I have trouble
The willow branch keeps me alive
it will be there when I die.

Using the index cards, Linh wrote this revision of her poem:

The Willow Branch

The willow branch has magical leaves.
It blows through the cold wind.
The ghosts fly by the silent child.
The willow branch has magical leaves.
The lonely room cries for warmth.
A quiet baby laughs alone.
The moon passes by with the earth's turns.
The willow branch has magical light.

EDITING AND REWRITING EXERCISES

Exercise *Making a Poem Stronger*

1. Because editing a poem can feel threatening to students, WritersCorps teacher Chad Sweeney suggests starting with an editing activity that everyone

does together. Instead of choosing a student's poem, Chad brings in a drab piece of writing he has written for the occasion. The group works together to find more interesting words and line breaks.

2. Share "The Rain Genie"—an intentionally weak piece by Herman Waxflatter, Chad's alter ego—and ask students to write a second draft of the poem by giving it more interesting words (word switch) and by choosing where to break the line (line breaks). Feel free to write your own flat piece to use as an example.

3. Ask students to help Herman Waxflatter by making his poem more interesting. Use the words in the word-switch lists that follow to replace Herman's dull vocabulary.

The Rain Genie

People go down the sidewalk. Birds fly over. Cars go on the street. Rain falls on the street. Wind blows people's hair. So people go under a roof. I see an old man talking to a kid. He says, "I'm cold, please help me." The kid says, "What can I do?" So the man says, "Just smile, that's enough." Rain falls harder, and wind blows. The kid smiles as big as he can. The old man is a genie in disguise, so he becomes a wind and blows away. The kid has magical good luck all his life.

WORD-SWITCH LISTS

Words for Go, Walk, Fly Motion

stride	strut	scurry
stalk	skulk	saunter
meander	groove	ramble
slither	soar	wing
lurch	lunge	hurry
speed	race	crawl
wander	bob	float
swim	hustle	cruise
surf	roll	stumble
stagger	head	cross/crisscross
traverse	travel	swoop
launch	bound	gambol
skip	jog	sprint

Words for Go, Walk, Fly Motion (continued)

dart	ease	glide
dance	hike	clamor
gallop	stampede	bolt

Words for Say and Talk

croak	cry out	yell
bark	whisper	sigh
grunt	dictate	repeat
question	wheeze	hiss
reply	purr	blurt
chuckle	snicker	giggle
laugh	cough	shout
demand	explain	implore
wheedle	whimper	retort
project	sing	interrupt
stammer	stutter	chant
intone	croon	keen
wail	screech	chirp
hiccup	belch	burp

Words for Up, Down Motion

plummet	rise	lift
float	ascend	descend
elevate	scale	sink
drop	fall	rain
cascade	precipitate	lower
hail	parachute	raise
slide	climb	jump
leap	reach	stoop

Words for Contact

reflect	ricochet	collide
shatter	jostle	bump
nudge	press	push

ruffle	drag	scrape
slide	tangle	rub
strike	rescue	join
melt together	meld	batter
craft	sculpt	carve
dampen	rust	pierce
cut	slice	protect
shelter	enliven	hold
inspire	scratch	squeeze
crack	hug	nestle
wrestle	embrace	bounce
shake	jolt	wrap

Words for Color

rose (red)	indigo (blue)	azure (blue)
rust	copper	bronze
topaz (yellow)	ivory (white)	obsidian (black)
coal	ebony (black)	emerald (green)
ruby	sienna	flame
violet	blush (pink)	bruise
moss	mauve	amethyst (deep purple)
clay	lavender	frost
midnight	plum	lemon
sapphire (blue)	turquoise	amber (golden)
smoke	charcoal (dark gray)	jade (green)
olive	brick	poppy
sage	opal	crimson (red)
slate gray	dove gray	ash gray

Exercise Read Aloud

Read the student's poem, story, or essay out loud so that the writer can hear its words. Often just hearing how the words sound gives the writer a sense of what he wants to clarify or make stronger.

Exercise Constructive Feedback

1. Ask each student to read aloud to the group a piece that he or she has written.

2. Allow each student to decide and then tell the group whether he or she wants constructive feedback that notes aspects of the work that the author might improve or just positive feedback.

3. After the student reads, go around the circle and ask each person to say one thing he or she likes about the piece, one thing the writer might change, and one thing the listener didn't understand. If the reader wants only positive feedback, the other students will say only what they liked about the piece.

Exercise Line Breaks

1. Type students' poems with attention to line breaks, revising these line breaks to improve the poem.

2. Hand these revised pieces back to their authors, talking about line breaks and your reasons for the choices you made. Let students know that this is an experiment that allows you to share more information about line but that the final choice about line breaks remains theirs.

3. Ask students to go over what you've typed. Do they agree with your choices? Make time to check in with each student one-on-one. Getting a sense of good line breaks often allows new poets to see other changes they might want to make to their work.

Exercise Eliminate Clichés

1. Write a piece yourself that is filled with clichés. Share the writing with the class and have your students point out as a group each overused image or word.

2. Then ask students to work on their own poems or stories, underlining every cliché.

3. Ask the writer to find a fresher image for these words or lines.

Exercise *Use a Checklist*

1. Give students a checklist with particulars for revision, such as the one by WritersCorps teacher Chad Sweeney.

2. Ask students to use the checklist as a way to revise their poems.

   ❏ Title and name: Check your title and how your name is written. Are they OK?

   ❏ Read the poem out loud and listen for places to change or add new ideas.

   ❏ Read it through carefully, looking for any part that needs to be made more interesting.

   ❏ Note repeated words, such as *beautiful, good, big*. If a word appears many times, please find a different word to make the poem more interesting.

   ❏ Please think of some new lines for the poem, to continue what you've already started. New lines can be in the middle of the poem or at the end, anywhere you have a new idea.

   ❏ Add new details to make a line stronger.

   ❏ Notice line breaks and shape. Decide how you want the poem to be shaped. To show a line break, use the slash (/). "The summer / is a green chair" therefore becomes:

     The summer

     is a green chair.

   ❏ Do you like the ending? The ending can summarize what your poem is about, or it can jump into a new idea. You decide.

EDITING STUDENT WRITING FOR PUBLICATION

Teachers often have to edit their students' work for publication. WritersCorps teachers suggest that when you edit young writers you not rewrite the piece. Although you might be tempted to impose your voice, your writing style, and your diction and syntax on a young writer's work, it is important for the writing itself and for the student's sense of his or her own work to preserve the piece's integrity.

Generally, we suggest that you correct spelling, typographical errors, and gross grammatical or syntactical mistakes; also note any words or lines that seem unclear to you as a reader. Try whenever possible to review your edits with the student so that he or she has an opportunity to agree or disagree with your changes. This step is critical because it conveys to your students that you respect them and their writing and that you understand that they, not you, are the creators of their work.

Exercise Editing Conferences

1. Type a student's work without editing anything other than spelling.

2. Check in one-on-one with the student, giving the whole group an art activity to work on as you meet individually with each youth.

3. In these conferences edit the piece with the young writer. Tell the student what you like about the piece and discuss ways that you think he or she can improve it. If you're editing a poem, for example, you can talk about line breaks, imagery, rhythm, word choice, and so forth.

Further Reading

Siegler, Alan. "A Few Notes on Revision." In Ron Padgett and Bill Zavatsky (eds.), *The Whole Word Catalogue 2.* New York: Teachers & Writers Collaborative, 1987.

Willis, Meredith Sue. "Deep Revision." In Christopher Edgar and Ron Padgett (eds.), *Educating the Imagination: Essays and Ideas for Teachers and Writers.* New York: Teachers & Writers Collaborative, 2000.

Appendix

THE TEACHERS OF THE SAN FRANCISCO WRITERSCORPS 1994–2004

Chrissy Anderson-Zavala
Cathy Arellano
Ellis Avery
Alegria Barclay
Stephen Beachy
Cherie Bombardier
Godhuli Bose
Tom Centolella
Carrie Chang
Elizebeth Chávez
Justin Chin
Eric Chow
Jorge Cortiñas
Leslie Davis
Colette DeDonato
Victor Diaz
Aja Couchois Duncan
Rebekah Eisenberg
Mahru Elahi
Ananda Esteva
Kathy Evans
Sauda Garrett
Russell Reza-Khaliz
   Gonzaga
Toussaint Haki

Susanna Hall
Lenore Harris
Donna Ho
LeCurtiss Hubbard
Uchechi Kalu
Carrie Kartman
Melissa Klein
Katherine LeRoy
Jaime Lujan
Margot Lynn
Michelle Matz
Scott Meltsner
Elizabeth Riva Meyer
D. Scott Miller
maiana minahal
Peter Money
Danielle Montgomery
Kimberley Nelson
Hoa Nguyen
Sharon O'Brien
Beto Palomar
Ishle Yi Park
Steve Parks
Andrew Pearson
Elissa Perry

Michelle Phillips
Marcos Ramirez
Christina Ramos
Victoria Rosales
Yiskah Rosenfeld
Andrew Saito
Jime Salcedo-Malo
Johnna Schmidt
Margaret Schulze
Alison Seevak
Christopher Sindt
giovanni singleton
Chad Sweeney
Luis Syquia
Penina Taesali
Peter Tamaribuchi
Lynnell Thomas
JoNelle Toriseva
Elsie Washington
Chris West
Marvin K. White
Canon Wing
William Wylie
Gloria Yamato
Tara Youngblood

WRITERSCORPS SITES 1994–2004

ArtSpan/Inner City Public Art Projects
   for Youth
Balboa High School
Bay High School
Bridges/Youth for Service
Career Resources Development Center
Center for Young Women's
   Development
Central City Hospitality House
Chinatown Youth Center
Chinese Progressive Association
Columbia Park Boys and Girls Club–
   Excelsior Branch
Drama DIVAS
Ella Hill Hutch Community Day School
Everett Middle School
Five Keys Charter School
Florence Crittenton Services
Galileo High School
Gateway High School
Gilman Playground
Girls After School Academy
Guerrero House
Horace Mann Middle School
Hospitality House
Huckleberry House
Ida B. Wells High School
Instituto Familiar de la Raza
International Studies Academy
Jamestown Community Center
John O'Connell Technical High School

Jovenes Unidos
Lakeshore Alternative Elementary
   School
Latinas in Theater
Lavender Youth Recreation and
   Information Center
Loco Bloco
Log Cabin Ranch
McAteer High School
Mercy Services
Mission Annex #2
Mission Girls
Mission High School
Newcomer High School
Office of Samoan Affairs
Phoenix Middle School
Project Ace/Wajumbe Cultural
   Institution
Recreation Center for the Handicapped
San Francisco Community School
San Francisco Educational Services
San Francisco Public Library
Teatro Ng Tanan
Tenderloin After School Program
Vietnamese Youth Development Center
Visitacion Valley Middle School
Woodside Learning Center
Youth Guidance Center
Youth Treatment and Education Center
YWCA Western Addition Center

For more information, contact:

WritersCorps
San Francisco Arts Commission
25 Van Ness Ave., Suite 240
San Francisco, CA 94102
415/252–4655
http://www.writerscorps.org

OTHER BOOKS BY WRITERSCORPS

Believe Me, I Know (WritersCorps Books, 2002)
City of One (Aunt Lute Books, 2004)
Curves on a Sidewalk Street (WritersCorps Books, 1997)
Flavors of the City (WritersCorps Books, 1995)
Jump (WritersCorps Books, 2001)
Lessons Along the Way (WritersCorps Books, 2001)
Paint Me Like I Am (HarperCollins, 2003)
Same Difference (WritersCorps Books, 1998)
Smart Mouth (WritersCorps Books, 2000)
What It Took for Me to Get Here (WritersCorps Books, 1999)
Word from the (415) (WritersCorps Books, 1996)

INDEX

.